At Issue

| Drunk Driving

Other Books in the At Issue Series:

At Issue

Drunk Driving

Tamara Thompson, Book Editor

GREENHAVEN PRESS

An imprint of Thomson Gale, a part of The Thomson Corporation

Detroit • New York • San Francisco • New Haven, Conn. • Waterville, Maine • London

Christine Nasso, *Publisher*
Elizabeth Des Chenes, *Managing Editor*

© 2008 The Gale Group.

For more information, contact:
Greenhaven Press
27500 Drake Rd.
Farmington Hills, MI 48331-3535
Or you can visit our Internet site at http://www.gale.com

LIBRARY OF CONGRESS CATALOGING-IN-PUBLICATION DATA

Drunk Driving / Tamara Thompson, book editor.
    p. cm. -- (At issue)
Includes bibliographical references and index.
ISBN-13: 978-0-7377-3683-0 (hardcover)
ISBN-13: 978-0-7377-3684-7 (pbk.)
1. Drunk driving--United States. 2. Drunk driving--United States--Prevention.
I. Thompson, Tamara.
    HE5620.D72D784 2008
    363.12'5140973--dc22

                                                        2007029301

ISBN-10: 0-7377-3683-6 (hardcover)
ISBN-10: 0-7377-3684-4 (pbk.)

Printed in the United States of America
10 9 8 7 6 5 4 3 2 1

Contents

Introduction

The death of one little girl forever changed how both American society and its legal system view drunk driving. In 1980, Candy Lightner's thirteen-year-old daughter, Cari, was killed by a drunk hit-and-run driver as she walked down a suburban street in California. The driver, who had four prior drunk driving arrests, received a two-year prison term but served his time via a work program and a halfway house. Outraged by the lenient sentence, Lightner launched Mothers Against Drunk Driving (MADD), hoping to redefine drunk driving as a serious crime and advocate for stronger laws, enforcement, and prevention. Begun as a grassroots group with donations from victims and a $65,000 grant from the National Highway Traffic Safety Administration (NHTSA), MADD has grown to include approximately six hundred chapters and two million members/supporters worldwide. MADD has been highly influential in shaping the nation's alcohol policies, and its efforts have contributed to the passage of more than 2,300 anti–drunk driving laws. According to NHTSA statistics, alcohol-related traffic fatalities have dropped 44 percent since the year MADD was founded—from 30,429 in 1980 to 17,941 in 2006.

Based on resesearch that showed young people were overrepresented in drunk driving fatalities, MADD's first legislative effort was to increase the drinking age to twenty-one nationwide. Because states set their own alcohol laws, the minimum age at the time varied among states. MADD lobbied heavily for a nationwide standard, and in 1984 Senator Frank Lautenberg of New Jersey proposed an amendment to a Senate transportation bill calling for states to raise their minimum drinking age to twenty-one within two years or lose 10 percent of their federal highway funds. It provided financial incentives for states to set mandatory sentencing laws.

The bill passed, despite objections that it unduly expanded the power of the federal government; subverted the right of states to set their own alcohol policies; and, in effect, blackmailed states into compliance by withholding federal money. Then-president Ronald Reagan signed the bill, and by 1988 all states had increased their minimum drinking age to twenty-one. That same year, twenty-seven people were killed in the nation's worst drunk-driving accident when a drunk driver plowed into a church bus filled with youths in Carrollton, Kentucky.

Winning a major victory with the Lautenberg amendment and attracting increased public support because of the Kentucky bus tragedy, MADD turned its efforts toward reducing the blood alcohol concentration (BAC) at which it is legal to drive. BAC is the amount of alcohol in the body, expressed as grams of alcohol per deciliter of blood, typically measured with a breath or blood test. A study by R. F. Borkenstein in 1964 showed that accident rates increase as BACs increase. Based on his work, some states already had BAC limits of .08 or .10 percent, but there was no national standard—some states had no limit at all. In arguing that a nationwide .08 BAC standard would save lives, MADD cited a study by the Insurance Institute for Highway Safety that showed people with BACs between .05 and .09 were 11 times more likely to die in an accident than those not drinking. Also, research from Boston University showed that in five states, fatalities of those who had BACs of .08 or higher dropped significantly faster in states that had .08 BAC laws rather than .10.

Believing a .08 threshold would unfairly penalize social drinkers, the alcohol industry vigorously opposed the law with research and statistics of its own—as well as more than $35 million in contributions to lawmakers and governors in 33 states, according to the citizens' lobbying group Common Cause. Yet in 1999, Lautenberg again presented a bill that tied state compliance with a national .08 BAC standard to federal purse strings. Then-president Bill Clinton signed the bill in 2000, and all states had to enact .08 BAC laws by 2004 or lose federal highway construction funds. All states have now [as of 2007] complied.

Critics argue that since drivers with BACs of .10 or higher account for nearly 80 percent of all alcohol-related fatalities, focusing on drivers who pose a minimal safety threat means fewer resources go to stopping the hard-core drunks who are the real problem. One of those critics is Candy Lightner, the founding mother of MADD. Lightner believes MADD has lost its focus and is pursuing a misguided war against social drinking, not drunk driving. She left the organization in 1985 to work as a lobbyist against the .08 effort. According to Lightner, MADD "has become far more neo-prohibitionist than I had ever wanted or envisioned . . . I didn't start MADD to deal with alcohol. I started MADD to deal with the issue of drunk driving . . . I worry that the movement I helped create has lost direction."

One reason for MADD's shift in focus may be that after steadily declining throughout the 1980s and 90s, alcohol-related deaths have reached a plateau, varying little since 2000 even as both the number of cars on the road and miles driven have increased. Struggling to remain relevant, MADD has set a new goal to "completely eliminate drunk driving" by making it impossible to drink and then drive. The group is currently advocating ignition interlocks as a way to achieve that goal. These devices analyze BAC and can prevent a vehicle from starting if the driver has consumed even a tiny amount of alcohol. The driver must breathe into the device before starting the vehicle and again while driving whenever the machine asks. Judges in many states require repeat drunk drivers to install interlocks as part of their sentences, but MADD wants it to be mandatory nationwide for even first-time offenders. The group has stated publicly that eventually it would like to see all new vehicles equipped with the devices. Critics maintain that interlocks are inaccurate, easily fooled, and may be dangerous because drivers are asked to conduct breath tests while driving. It remains to be seen whether interlocks will help further reduce drunk-driving accidents, and whether the public will welcome the devices or view them as an unacceptable government intrusion.

A similar concern arises with sobriety checkpoints, roadblocks at which police randomly stop motorists and screen them for signs of alcohol impairment. Because officers check drivers who have not obviously violated any laws, many people believe that roadblocks are unconstitutional because they violate the Fourth Amendment's protection from unreasonable search and seizure. Courts in at least ten states have ruled sobriety checkpoints illegal in their jurisdictions; others routinely conduct them. While very few people stopped by checkpoints are arrested as drunk drivers, their high visibility makes them good education and prevention tools, officials say. Critics argue that instead of stopping the worst offenders, checkpoints primarily snare drivers at lower BACs who are not significantly impaired. Says Lightner: "Police ought to be concentrating their resources on arresting drunk drivers—not those drivers who happen to have been drinking."

MADD and its opponents differ substantially regarding how far the government should go to prevent drunk driving. Finding a balance between public safety and individuals' rights continues to be a key issue in regulating and enforcing drunk driving laws. The authors in *At Issue: Drunk Driving* discuss these issues and examine the social and legal implications of drunk driving. In addition, victims and offenders share their personal stories from both sides of drunk driving tragedies.

1

Drunk Driving Is a Serious National Problem

David J. Hanson, Ph.D.

David J. Hanson is a widely published alcohol researcher who regularly speaks in the media as an alcohol expert. He is professor emeritus of sociology at the State University of New York at Potsdam.

Drunk driving is a problem that has no single or simple solution. Automatic license revocation and jail time appear to be the best deterrents for most drivers. There are many new approaches to reducing drunk driving—such as making the vehicles of offenders identifiable and expanding alcohol server training programs—but the effectiveness of these ideas has not been adequately studied. Many of the things that deter typical drivers have no impact on those with high blood alcohol concentrations (BAC); high BAC drivers are responsible for most alcohol-related traffic deaths. Injuries and death caused by drunk driving are completely preventable. The key things to remember are to never drive a vehicle after drinking alcohol and never get into a car with anyone who has been drinking. It is always safest not to drink and drive.

Driving while either intoxicated or drunk is dangerous and drivers with high blood alcohol content (BAC) are at increased risk of car accidents, highway injuries and vehicular deaths. Prevention measures evaluated include license suspension or revocation, impounding or confiscating vehicle plates,

David J. Hanson, Ph.D., "Drinking & Driving," *Alcohol Problems*, http://www2.potsdam .edu/alcohol-info/DrinkingAndDriving.html. Reproduced by permission.

enforcing open container bans, increasing penalties such as fines or jail for drunk driving, mandating education for young people, and lowering legal BACs. Also discussed are safety seat belts, air bags, designated drivers, and effective practical ways to stay sober.

Every single injury and death caused by drunk driving is totally preventable. Unfortunately, over twenty percent of all traffic fatalities in the United States each year are caused by drunk drivers. Thus, drunk driving remains a serious national problem that tragically affects thousands of victims annually.

It's easy to forget that dry statistics represent real people and real lives. . . .

Automatic license revocation appears to be the single most effective measure to reduce drunk driving.

Most drivers who have had something to drink have low blood alcohol content or concentration (BAC) and few are involved in fatal crashes. On the other hand, while only a few drivers have BACs higher than .15, many of those drivers have fatal crashes.

- The average BAC among fatally injured drinking drivers is .17.

- Almost half of fatally injured drinking drivers have a BAC of .20 or over (which is twice the legal limit in most jurisdictions).

High BAC drivers tend to be male, aged 25–35, and have a history of DWI convictions and polydrug abuse.

Effective Deterrents to Drunk Driving

Drunk driving, like most other social problems, resists simple solutions. However, there are a number of actions, each of which can contribute toward a reduction of the problem:

- Automatic license revocation appears to be the single most effective measure to reduce drunk driving. Not only is license revocation effective, but we should remember that driving is a privilege, not a right. Just as we do not license those who lack eyesight, we should not hesitate to revoke the licenses of those who lack the good judgment not to drive drunk.

- Automatic license revocation along with a mandatory jail sentence appears to be even more effective than just automatic license revocation.

- Passing mandatory alcohol and drug testing in fatal crashes would promote successful prosecution of drunk and drugged drivers.

The National Highway Traffic Safety Administration [NTSA] estimates that 18–20% of injured drivers are using drugs and although drinking is on the decline, drugging is on the increase. However, this figure appears to be much too low. For example:

- A study by the Addiction Research Foundation of vehicle crash victims who tested positive for either legal or illegal substances found that just 15% had consumed only alcohol.

- A Tennessee study found that over half of reckless drivers not intoxicated by alcohol were intoxicated by other substances and noted that "Studies of injured drivers suggest that driving under the influence of drugs other than alcohol is a growing cause of traffic injuries in the United States."

New Approaches to the DUI Problem
Promising but inadequately evaluated measures include:

- Marking the license plate to indicate ownership in the family of someone whose driver's license is suspended or revoked for alcohol offenses.

- Impounding or confiscating the plates of vehicles used in the offense of drunk driving.

- Impounding and confiscating vehicles used in the commission of drunk driving.

- Passing and enforcing bans on open containers would reduce drunk driving by deterring drinking while driving. Surprisingly, 22 states have no open container laws.

- Imposing graded or multi-tiered penalties based on BAC at the time of arrest.

- Expanding alcohol server training programs.

- Restricting nighttime driving by young people. This appears to be effective in those states with such restrictions.

- Requiring every state to provide adequate information on alcohol and driving to prospective drivers and adequately testing them on the subject in their driver's exams. In too many states, the subject is given only brief mention and seven states do not include any information or testing in the process of obtaining a driver's license.

All of these very promising measures should be rigorously evaluated scientifically to determine their potential contribution to improving safety.

The risk of collision for high BAC drivers is several hundred times higher than for a non-drinking driver.

Some Penalties with Little Effect
Measures of little or no value include:

- Jail or prison sentences for alcohol offenses, in spite of their great popularity, appear to be of little value in deterring high BAC drivers.

- Such sentences may deter low BAC drinkers, but such drivers are not the problem. Incarceration is probably ineffective with high BAC drivers, who tend to be alcohol dependent individuals with very serious problems who need treatment.

- The perception of swift and certain punishment is more important than severity.

- Large fines (for example $500) would have little deterrent effect, according to a nation-wide study.

- Increasing the cost of alcohol with a ten percent tax would have virtually no impact on reducing drunk driving. Why would it? Both research and common sense suggest that heavy drinkers are not deterred by cost. However, increasing the cost would tend to discriminate against lower income consumers and create other problems of unknown magnitude.

Protect yourself and others by never driving if you think, or anyone else thinks, that you might have had too much to drink.

Improved roads and vehicles can contribute significantly to increased highway safety. Technological improvements include raised lane markers, which are easier to see and also emit a startling sound when a tire wanders over them. Similarly corrugations along the edges of roads emit a sound when driven over, thus alerting inattentive drivers to their inappropriate location. Wider roads, improved street and highway lighting, break-away sign posts, brake lights positioned at eye level, door crash bars, and many other improvements can save lives and are cost-effective.

Protect Yourself

While society has done much to improve highway safety, you can do much to protect yourself.

Don't drink and drive and don't ride with anyone who has too much to drink. Remember, it is usually themselves and their passengers who are harmed by drunk drivers. The risk of collision for high BAC drivers is several hundred times higher than for a non-drinking driver.

Volunteer to be a designated driver.

Always use a safety seat belt. . . .

Never condone or approve of excessive alcohol consumption. Intoxicated behavior is potentially dangerous and never amusing.

Don't ever let your friends drive drunk. Take their keys, have them stay the night, have them ride home with someone else, call a cab, or do whatever else is necessary—but don't let them drive! . . .

Protect others and yourself by never driving if you think, or anyone else thinks, that you might have had too much to drink. It's always best to use a designated driver.

The Good News

We can do it! While we must do even more to reduce drunk driving, we have already accomplished a great deal.

- The U.S. has a low traffic fatality rate (drunk, as well as sober) and is a very safe nation in which to drive. And it's been getting safer for decades. There is now only about one death (including the deaths of bicyclists, motorcyclists, pedestrians, auto drivers, and auto passengers) per fifty million vehicle miles traveled.

- Alcohol-related traffic fatalities have dropped from 60% of all traffic deaths in 1982 down to 41% in 2002 (the most recent year for which such statistics are available).

- Alcohol-related traffic fatalities per vehicle miles driven has also dropped dramatically—from 1.64 deaths per 100 million miles traveled in 1982 down to 0.61 in 2002 (the latest year for which such statistics are available).

- Alcohol-related crash fatalities have fallen 1/3 since 1982, but traffic deaths NOT associated with alcohol have jumped 43% during the same time. We're winning the battle against alcohol-related traffic fatalities, but losing the fight against traffic deaths that are not alcohol-related.

Remember, don't ever, ever drive if you, or anyone else, thinks that you may have had too much to drink. And don't let anyone else. That includes reporting drivers who may be drunk. It's always safest not to drink and drive.

2

Drunk Driving Is a Life Sentence for Many Victims

Mothers Against Drunk Driving

Founded in 1980, MADD's mission is to stop drunk driving, support the victims of this violent crime and prevent underage drinking. MADD is a 501c(3) non-profit, grassroots organization with approximately 400 affiliates and 2 million members and supporters nationwide.

While drunk drivers who cause injuries or deaths may spend some time behind bars as punishment for their actions, for their victims the accident can often be a life sentence. Drunk driving has lifelong ramifications for those who are injured and who must live the rest of their lives with pain, disability, isolation, medical bills, or the loss of loved ones. While drunk-driving offenders can usually reclaim a normal life after their eventual release from jail, victims may never regain the normalcy that was taken from them so abruptly.

For many victims, a drunk driving crash is just the beginning. Years of emotional, physical and financial ramifications are the unjust burden these innocent motorists bear.

Imprisoned for 12 years, Sherry Catarcio longs for release from the sentence of drunk driving. Oh, she never drove drunk—the man who did that got nine months in jail with work release privileges. Nor was she a passenger when the offender, who had been drinking all day, hit her husband's car head-on. But her punishment has been long. And her prison is her home.

Mothers Against Drunk Driving (MADD), "Unjust Consequences," *Driven Magazine*, Spring 2003. Reproduced by permission.

"You might as well put bars on the windows, because I never get to leave," Sherry says, referring to her New Brighton, Pa., residence where she struggles, cries and provides around-the-clock care for her husband Jerry. This has been her life since the day in 1991 when a drunk driver stole their dreams.

"Jerry was a few minutes from home. He never knew what hit him," she says, remembering the helplessness that suffocated her when a nurse handed her a bag containing 35 cents, a bloodstained tennis shoe and a mangled watch. "We weren't sure he would make it," she says. "Unfortunately, he did."

What sounds like a heartless statement is really the reflective longing of a wife whose heart breaks every time her husband howls in pain.

"Since the crash, Jerry has been unable to talk," Sherry says. "He cannot eat or drink. I bathe him, shave him and administer his IV. I take care of his bladder and bowel control. All he can do on his own is breathe."

And cry out in pain.

For 12 years, Jerry has suffered excruciating pain, emitting sounds Sherry likens to the cries of a wounded animal. Meanwhile, more than a decade of isolation, financial strain, health problems and unrelenting daily demands are taking their toll on Sherry.

"I don't get to enjoy anything outside this house because Jerry needs 24/7 care. I miss my grandchildren's softball games and awards ceremonies. There are times I'm just so tired and I know tomorrow is going to be the same as it was today, I'm just holding on," Sherry says.

She is not alone.

Her fate is shared by people all over the country—people living with the long-term consequences of drunk driving. They are the ones who bear the daily and unjust burden of someone else's decision to drink and drive.

The Ripples Effect

Few are as well acquainted with the lifelong ramifications of drunk driving as 51-year-old Scott Alan Keeler, president of MADD Kalamazoo County, Mich., and member of the MADD Michigan Public Policy Committee. In 1962, a drunk driver broadsided the Keelers' family car. His mom died instantly, his father suffered serious injuries and his sister was thrown from the car. Rescue workers found Scott, then 10 years old, pinned in the back seat.

Scott sustained traumatic brain injury—a condition that can impair cognitive and physical abilities and cause behavioral or emotional disturbances. Because of his brain injury, Scott still suffers from severe limitations in mobility on his left side as well as short-term memory loss and, sometimes, a lack of inhibition.

But what people first notice is the way he talks.

Stilted and sometimes indecipherable, his speech sets him apart in a fast-paced world that prizes quick communication.

"People have judged me to be mentally retarded or drunk. Or they think I have cerebral palsy," Scott says. "They finish my sentences or just cut me off altogether."

It's not something you just get over. . . . Drunk driving changes your whole life. The ripples never stop.

Because of his limitations, he has had trouble finding almost any job. Though he now has a good job working 12 hours a week as a community outreach advocate for the Disability Resource Center of Southwestern Michigan, previous workplaces have delivered cruel blows.

From dishwasher and custodian to teacher aide and pharmacy technician, Scott has been scrutinized and belittled on the job.

"People judge my gait and the way I speak," Scott says. "One boss even asked my wife—instead of me—if she thought I could do the job."

In 1980, a neuropsychologist assessed Scott's intelligence as questionable. Scott proved his intelligence by earning a master's degree in social work. His larger goal now is to prove how long lasting the effects of drunk driving are.

He tells audiences about his ordeal that began in a coma with a fight for his life and continued into adolescence with his struggle for social survival. Rejected by his father's new wife, he was placed in foster care—missing his mom, alienated from family and without friends.

Now, four full decades later, he fights for normalcy; the kind of normalcy his offender easily obtained following 208 days—served only on weekends—in Michigan's Genesee County Jail.

Scott's wife Stephanie serves alongside him in the fight against drunk driving in her role as chairwoman of MADD Michigan. Together, they face financial burdens, health insurance hassles and a brick wall of social disadvantages.

"It's not something you just get over," Scott says, inviting anyone who believes otherwise to walk in his $250 shoes—shoes that he has had to have custom made since the 1962 crash that changed even the length of his legs. "Drunk driving changes your whole life. The ripples never stop."

While some drunk driving victims must learn to go on living, others endure the tragedy of saying goodbye.

'Don't Tell Me He Was Drunk'

In Pensacola, Fla., Jerry Fifer is settling into the rigors of life after an alcohol-related crash. A retired Navy Cryptologic Technician, Jerry was already acquainted with the tragic consequences of drunk driving. Drunk drivers caused the deaths of both his high-school girlfriend in 1978 and his brother-in-law in 1994.

That's why his first words following his head-on crash were, "Tell me the guy had a heart attack. Tell me he had a blown tire. But don't tell me he was drunk."

The driver who hit Jerry's prized 1987 Jeep in Sept. 2000 was indeed intoxicated with a .22 percent blood alcohol level. He completed one year of work-release jail time in March and is now on probation for four years.

Meanwhile, Jerry has endured 14 surgical procedures, skin grafts, infections and a grueling rehabilitation regimen to get him moving again following multiple head injuries, broken bones and a nearly severed leg.

Because of a circulatory problem, he experiences severe inflammation in his right leg. A half-day outing lands him in bed, where it can take nine hours for his extremely swollen lower leg to return to normal size.

And then there's the collateral damage.

A steel rod inserted in his right femur, along with a steel screw in his right hip, and three steel plates and screws in his left forearm are all used to hold broken and cracked bones in place. They will remain there forever.

He has also developed diabetes and two hernias. Because he is unable to work due to the crash, he has teetered on the brink of bankruptcy and his credit is shot. He constantly fights depression and his marriage has been shaken to the core.

"I would sit near windows, in tears, watching my wife mow the yard, fix fences or take care of our four dogs. She works, takes care of me and struggles with the bills. The pressure is enormous," Jerry says.

Though the crash was not his fault, the marital conflicts have been many.

"There were times it would get so ugly I would wish I had died. And the kicker was, I couldn't even get up to walk out of the room to avoid a confrontation."

His sense of humor masks the depression he often feels.

During his long recovery, Jerry was confined to his bed or a wheelchair. Home alone while his wife was at work, he would get frustrated at not being able to do the things he used to do. "I'd drop something—the phone or a glass of water—and I couldn't get to it. I would just weep and think to myself, 'How did I wind up like this?'" Jerry says, adding that isolation adds to his despair. "My friends don't come over as often. When they do, I feel like a wallflower. It all changed so fast."

The Beginning of the End

While some drunk driving victims must learn to go on living, others endure the tragedy of saying goodbye.

I think of things like: What if God gave Kimberly the ability to cure cancer? But now, we'll never know.

Sherry Hampton-Sands began the morning of June 10, 2000, in the Apple Valley, Calif., home she shared with her 26-year-old daughter Wendy and six-year-old granddaughter Kimberly. Heading off to a friend's birthday party, Kimberly asked, "Grandma, do you want to go to the party too?"

"No, baby, maybe another time," Sherry said.

Another time would never come. A drunk driver travelling 90 mph in a pickup truck ran a stop sign and broadsided Wendy's sedan. Wendy was instantly killed and Kimberly struggled to breathe for two minutes before she died.

Sherry describes that day as the beginning of the end. In addition to trying to cope with the unbearable sorrow over the death of her daughter and granddaughter, Sherry was fired from her 13-year job because of the time off she needed to take to grieve. Her $40,000 annual income was slashed to

$758 a month in Social Security benefits. She suffers post-traumatic stress disorder and her doctor deemed her unable to work. Eventually, she had to let go of her house because she could no longer afford it.

Other effects manifest themselves in more subtle ways.

"I have backed off from my siblings," says Sherry, one of nine kids in a very close-knit family. "If I am too close to them and I hear a siren, I think one of them has been involved in a crash."

As if the sorrow and fear are not enough, Sherry has dealt with court problems that border on cruelty.

"We were in court 39 times and nothing happened. The offender fired his first and second attorneys and they always had to re-do this or re-do that," Sherry says. Then, unbelievably, she received subpoenas from the district attorney's office for her dead daughter and granddaughter to testify. They came on what would have been Wendy's 28th birthday.

Referencing Edvard Munch's portrait "The Scream," Sherry says, "That's how I feel inside all the time, but I'm afraid to let it out because I'm afraid it won't stop." Sherry's son Matt states that three people really died that day: Wendy, Kimberly and Sherry.

Living in a controlled rage, Sherry goes through life's motions, but finds little joy in the things she used to do. Mostly, she misses her daughter and granddaughter and wonders who they might have become. "I think of things like: What if God gave Kimberly the ability to cure cancer? But now, we'll never know."

You tell me which one of your kids you can do without. When we buried Amy, we buried a part of us.

We Buried a Part of Us

Pam Tripp of New Tazewell, Tenn., knows what those kinds of haunting questions are like, which is why she leaves the TV on all the time—even when she goes to sleep. "If I have noise, I don't think. If it's quiet, I think too much," she says.

Pam and her husband David's 17-year-old daughter Amy was killed by a drunk driver on Dec. 17, 1995. In cruel irony, it was the first night they had ever let her stay out past her 11 p.m. curfew—a time they set to help ensure she was home before statistics show that the majority of drunk drivers are on the road.

Hit head-on by a car driven by a 45-year-old man who had to have a beer bottle removed from between his legs, Amy's car had a trunk full of Christmas presents that were never delivered.

"We don't do a [Christmas] tree anymore," says Pam, adding that the unopened presents from 1995 rest in a curio case in Amy's bedroom. "I can't imagine at Christmastime not ever having that awful dark feeling I have."

People have told Pam to put the fatal crash behind her. "I had a person tell me that one day, and I said to her, 'You tell me which one of your kids you can do without.' When we buried Amy, we buried a part of us."

Like so many other drunk driving victims, Pam had to leave her job, but not for reasons one might expect. She enjoyed her work as a legal secretary with the 8th Judicial public defender's office. But after Amy's crash, she could hardly stomach it because many of her office's clients were trying to beat drunk driving charges.

Meanwhile, David, a detective with the Union County Sheriff's Department, walked away from 25 years of law enforcement in 1998. "The first call he got when he went back to work after Amy's death was a wreck where three teens were killed. They had been drinking," Pam says. "After a while the job just started to eat at him, so he left."

David returned to detective work . . . , but he no longer works car crashes.

As for Pam, she describes herself as an emotional wreck who relies on antidepressants. She developed whooping cough after Amy died, had a tumor removed from her head in 1996 and had her colon removed in 2000. "It's been an ordeal," she says, adding that doctors say stress from her daughter's death has likely contributed to her health problems.

My girls don't smile as much. Their father has been taken away. He is living in my husband's body but he is not the same person.

Meanwhile, a circus of court proceedings has done little to assuage her stress.

It took four years, two judges and five hearings to get the offender in the state penitentiary. "Now he has filed a petition saying his lawyer was not effective and he was coerced into entering a guilty plea for vehicular homicide. It just never ends," Pam says.

One year after Amy was killed, a drunk driver hit Pam.

"I was on my way home at 4:30 p.m. I got so mad because it didn't kill me. How unfair it is for me to live when my Amy didn't," Pam says. "My heart is just broken."

Living with a Stranger

Tina Cook knows a different kind of heartbreak—the daily realization that the man she married is essentially a child trapped in a man's body. Hit by a 17-year-old, uninsured drunk driver in August 1999, her husband Gregg has suffered a fate shared by so many drunk driving victims. In addition to a broken neck and compressed spinal cord, he sustained traumatic brain injury.

"He's like a 250-pound toddler. He throws temper tantrums. He breaks things," Tina says. One day, the stress of watching his daughters—three active, squealing little girls ages six, seven and nine—caused his brain to short-circuit. "He just went in the closet, closed the door and fell asleep. He just shut his brain down because it was so overloaded," Tina says.

After that incident, Tina took her husband to a brain injury facility.

"The girls thought I was taking him to make him the way he was before. They thought they would get their daddy back. I had to tell them they weren't," she says, adding that adjusting to their "new daddy" has been hard. Multiple surgeries and the placement of supportive titanium plates in his neck cause Gregg to moan and groan in excruciating pain. His daughters often remain at arm's length.

"My girls don't smile as much. Their father has been taken away. He is living in my husband's body but he is not the same person," Tina says.

Meanwhile, the offender, who jumped bail and ran for about a year, was apprehended on Nov. 23, 2000—the Cooks' ninth wedding anniversary. He was sentenced to 10 years of probation and 180 days of "shock probation," prison time designed to shock or deter criminals from future offenses.

"He didn't get very much time because he was a first-time offender. But a family's life has been destroyed," Tina says.

Left to manage all the emotions, medications and finances, she has watched her middle-class suburban life disintegrate into a nightmare of daily calls from collection agencies. The Cooks make too much money to qualify for Medicaid and too little to make ends meet.

Laid off from her job in the aerospace industry after Sept. 11, 2001, Tina drew unemployment benefits for a year. Combining that with Gregg's $1,244 monthly disability check, they were scraping by. But her unemployment benefits have dried up. The medical bills are in the five digits, the mortgage payment on their home in an Austin, Texas, suburb is $1,000 a month and health insurance is $600—an expensive but vital cost because Gregg becomes violent if he's not on his medications.

"I just cashed out our 401K, but that is the last of the last. I'm going to have to sell the house," Tina says.

In lighter moments, Gregg reads to the girls and he and Tina joke around. "I'll call him the 'Six-million-dollar man' because by the time our lives have ended he will probably cost that much," she says.

But light moments are rare.

Exhausted from the burden of keeping collection agencies at bay, parenting three little girls and taking care of the man who once took care of her, Tina often falls asleep doing daily activities. "I don't know how long I can hold on," she says. "I have been holding onto an unraveling thread for so long—it's about to snap."

Forever Haunted

Tina's words echo the hard reality expressed by so many victims—victims of a crime that in every single case could have been prevented. That's the thing that will forever haunt Sherry Catarcio. Remember her, the one whose husband requires around-the-clock care for his every need?

By the accounts of several bar patrons, the driver who hit her husband's car was literally falling-down drunk before he got behind the wheel. Any number of people—including the bartender, who was the offender's sister—could have taken his keys away.

Now, Sherry just longs for the day when her husband will be released from his excruciating pain. "I hope he will sleep away peacefully. For his sake, I want it to be soon. There's nothing left of him now."

For her, the hurt caused by the thought of saying goodbye is surpassed only by the hell of watching Jerry live. "His bones are pressing against his skin. The liquid food that nourishes him has ulcerated his throat so that he bleeds and coughs it up. He is in constant pain," she says.

While her husband's passing might deliver them both from one prison, Sherry fears it will usher her into another. At 59, she has not been in the workplace for 12 years. She is on government disability because of debilitating back pain caused by the pushing and pulling required to daily maneuver her husband to and from bed. "I don't know what I'm going to do with my life. How will I live? At my age and in my health I can't just go back into the workplace," she says.

And Jerry can never go back to the way he was.

"This isn't something that heals," Sherry says. "If Jerry could ever have recovered to the point of being functional that would be one thing, but he lives in a vegetative state. If he would have died the night of the crash, I would have remembered him the way he was—a 6-foot 1-inch, 240-pound man who hunted, fished, and was very handsome and energetic. Now I'll remember him as a 120-pound skeleton of a man who fights so hard not to hurt. That is what drinking and driving does."

3

Anti–Drunk Driving Group Wants New Prohibition Era

James Nesci

James Nesci is an Arizona criminal defense attorney who specializes in defending serious drunk driving cases. He is a sustaining member of the National College for DUI Defense.

The nation's foremost anti-drunk driving group, Mothers Against Drunk Driving (MADD), has strayed from its original purpose. Instead of simply working to reduce drunk driving, the group is now pushing toward the total prohibition of alcohol. MADD distorts statistics to make the drunk driving problem seem much worse than it is, and to make DUI interventions appear more effective than they actually are. The group's current effort to require all vehicles to have ignition lock devices that prevent driving after any amount of alcohol will raise costs and unduly restrict personal freedoms. MADD's efforts are eroding Americans' Constitutional rights, and that effect is more dangerous than drunk driving will ever be.

MADD [Mothers Against Drunk Driving] is using bogus statistics to push its agenda of prohibition. It first tried to make people register beer kegs like guns. Now it wants all first-time DUI offenders to be required to have ignition interlock devices.

The group's intermediate goal is to have all new cars equipped with devices from the factory. Ultimately, MADD would have us repeat the failed social experiment called Pro-

James Nesci, "Guest Opinion: MADD Uses Bogus Stats to Chip Away Our Rights," *Arizona Daily Star*, December 7, 2006. Reproduced by permission of the author.

hibition. [The time from 1920 to 1933 when the U.S. Constitution outlawed the making, transportation, and sale of alcoholic beverages.]

Don't believe the hype. MADD falsely claims that there are 13,000 yearly "drunk driving" deaths. MADD uses statistics from the National Highway Traffic Safety Administration, which recorded over 13,000 "alcohol-related traffic fatalities," not drunken-driving deaths.

A true drunken-driving fatality years ago may now be a non-injury accident due solely to a more safe vehicle.

Statistics Are Faulty

An "alcohol-related traffic fatality" includes drunken drivers, drunken pedestrians run over by sober drivers, and traffic fatalities with any measurable amount of alcohol in the deceased's system. A measurable amount is 0.002 percent, which is one sip of light beer for a 175-pound man.

MADD attributes an average yearly decrease in drunken-driving fatalities to strict enforcement of DUI laws and ignition interlock devices. While this may be partially true, these are not the only reasons. Vehicles have become progressively more safe.

Thus, what would have been a true drunken-driving fatality years ago may now be a non-injury accident due solely to a more safe vehicle. The collective reasons for the statistical drop in fatalities cannot be separated.

The original intent behind drunken-driving laws has been lost with the advent of arbitrary laws that make it illegal to drive with a particular blood alcohol concentration. The original limits were lowered from 0.15 percent to 0.10 percent, then to 0.08 percent. Some states, such as Colorado, have a 0.05 percent limit for DWAI—driving with ability impaired.

Ignition Lock Technology Will Raise Costs

MADD is pushing to make it illegal for one to consume any amount of alcohol, then drive. Ignition interlocks will not let you drive at a 0.03 percent blood-alcohol concentration—that's less than one glass of wine for a 110-pound woman.

Ignition interlocks will drastically increase the cost of a new vehicle. The device may only cost about a thousand dollars, but when we shift the responsibility of sober driving from the driver to the car manufacturer and one of these devices fails, who will be liable?

Will your insurance company raise the rates for any car that does not have a device? Will MADD send a taxi and a bottle of ice water to you when you are stranded halfway between Yuma and Gila Bend in late July because the device malfunctioned and shut down your car for no reason?

The danger to ourselves created by drunken drivers on the road pales in comparison with the danger created by the loss of our Constitutional rights.

Constitutional Rights Are at Risk

The bottom line is that MADD is attempting to make legal behavior illegal with no rational basis for doing so. It is pushing for its goal of complete prohibition by chipping away at our constitutional freedoms by using bogus statistics and emotional arguments.

If you think that you have had too much to drink to drive, then don't drive. The danger to ourselves created by drunken drivers on the road pales in comparison with the danger created by the loss of our constitutional rights at the hands of MADD.

4

Drunk-Driving Laws Make Roads More Dangerous

Radley Balko

Radley Balko is a policy analyst at the Cato Institute, a libertarian research organization.

The nationwide standard for drunk driving—a blood alcohol content (BAC) of .08—is too low and is doing more harm than good. Drivers with a BAC of .10 or higher account for nearly 80 percent of all alcohol-related fatalities each year. Instead of stopping the worst offenders, sobriety checkpoints primarily snare drivers at lower BACs who are not significantly impaired. Focusing on drivers who do not pose a real safety threat means fewer resources go to stopping the hardcore drunks who are the real problem. This makes America's roads more dangerous overall. Congress should raise the national BAC standard for drunk driving so that enforcement efforts can be better focused and more effective.

Kudos to the D.C. Council, which recently voted in favor of a resolution by Carol Schwartz, at-large Republican, to nix the District's unjust "zero tolerance" policy of allowing police to arrest motorists who register any alcohol at all after stopping them for other offenses.

The Schwartz resolution was inspired by an article in *The Washington Post*, which found that hundreds of D.C. residents had been arrested for driving under the influence (DUI) with blood alcohol levels below .05, including some at as low as .01.

Radley Balko, "DC Forum: Lower DUI Threshold More Dangerous?" *Washington Times*, October 30, 2005. Reproduced by permission of the author.

The larger problem, however, is the fact that since 2000, the federal government has mandated a blanket .08 legal threshold for the entire country. We've now had five years of data to measure the effectiveness of the .08 standard, and the data strongly suggest that not only is the standard too low, but the resources we're expending to enforce it may actually be making our roadways more dangerous. Here's how:

Transportation Funding Depends on DUI Threshold

When President Clinton signed the .08 law in 2000, every state was forced to either comply with the law or give up millions of dollars in federal highway money. Critics at the time pointed to numerous studies showing that motorists aren't significantly impaired at .08, and that in fact, most drunk driving fatalities occur at .15 or higher. Lowering the national standard from .10 to .08, then, was a bit like lowering the speed limit from 55 to 50 to catch motorists who zip along at 100 miles per hour.

In 1992, the Supreme Court gave its consent to random sobriety checkpoint roadblocks, despite conceding that they are probably a violation of the Fourth Amendment. Writing for the majority, Chief Justice William Rehnquist ruled that the threat to highway safety posed by drunk driving justifies suspending our constitutional protection from illegal search and seizure, as well as our Fifth Amendment right against self-incrimination. Drunk driving activists seized on the ruling and moved to employ roadblocks all over the country.

Drunk Driving Deaths Continue to Rise

Critics of roadblocks and .08 predicted that (1) the lower standard would actually cause an increase in drunk driving deaths, as scarce law enforcement resources are diverted toward motorists who don't pose a real threat to highway safety and away from the "hardcore" drunks that do; and (2) these roadblocks will be set up under the guise of drunk driving, but will in effect become little more than revenue generators, as police use them to issue citations for any number of less serious infractions.

People with a blood alcohol content above .10 account for 77 percent of alcohol-related fatalities.

Both predictions have proven true. From 2000 to 2003, drunk-driving deaths began to inch upward again, after two decades of decline. In March of this year [2005], the National Transportation Safety Board conceded as much in a newsletter, warning that "Americans are more aware than ever before of the dangers of drinking and driving. Few realize, however, that drunk driving fatalities continue to rise—and that thousands of them are caused by extreme or repeat offenders known as 'hard core drinking drivers.'"

'Hardcore' Drunks Are the Worst Offenders

The release noted that these hardcore offenders produce 40 percent of traffic accidents, but comprise just 33 percent of arrests. If we look at fatalities, the numbers are worse: People with a blood alcohol content (BAC) above .10 account for 77 percent of alcohol-related fatalities (the average drunk driving fatality involves a BAC of .17). In other words, motorists with very high blood alcohol levels account for an increasing percentage of highway fatalities, but a decreasing percentage of arrests. Of course, the federal government still doesn't get it. The top bullet point in the NTSB's press release's action agenda was to install yet more "frequent and statewide sobriety checkpoints."

Last year the number of alcohol-related fatalities went down a bit. But deaths actually increased in states that use roadblocks. The overall drop came almost entirely from the handful of states that don't use roadblocks. Roadblocks are designed to catch motorists who aren't driving erratically enough to be caught by conventional means—and consequently, aren't as much of a threat. Given that the sites are generally well-publicized, hardcore drinkers know to avoid them.

The lower threshold is not only targeting motorists who aren't significantly impaired, it may well be making our roads more dangerous.

Roadblocks Are Money-Makers

Roadblocks have also turned into naked money-generators. A study of five Sacramento roadblocks found 22 suspected DUI arrests, but 315 citations and 215 vehicle confiscations for unrelated offenses. A newspaper account of a North Carolina roadblock reported 45 non-DWI offenses and just 3 suspected DWIs. A study of a recent San Diego roadblock found 1,169 stops, 27 citations, 10 vehicles impounded—and one DUI arrest. Here in D.C., police have been criticized for keeping a database of personal information collected from all motorists stopped at roadblocks—even those accused of no infraction at all. Many police departments have grown so frustrated with the process that they've given up roadblocks altogether, as well as the federal funding that comes with them.

Congress Should Revise DUI Standard

The D.C. Council was wise to scrap zero tolerance. And given the control Congress exerts over the District and the millions in federal dollars attached to it, it's probably unreasonable for the council to scrap its .08 standard, too. But even the Schwartz bill gives police officers discretion to arrest motorists between .05 and .079, a level of impairment studies show to be lower than having kids in the backseat. The council should correct this error.

In the larger picture, Congress should revisit its blanket .08 standard. The evidence so far suggests that the lower threshold is not only targeting motorists who aren't significantly impaired, it may well be making our roads more dangerous.

5

Sobriety Checkpoints Are Key to Preventing Drunk Driving

Rebecca Kanable

Rebecca Kanable is a freelance writer based in Wisconsin. She was previously an associate editor with Law Enforcement Technology, *a monthly magazine for law enforcement officers nationwide.*

The effort against drunk driving has reached a plateau. After declining significantly in the 1980s and 1990s, the number of alcohol-related traffic deaths has dropped very little over the past few years. Better drunk-driving prevention and enforcement efforts are needed to further reduce the number of fatalities. The most effective deterrent to drunk driving is frequently conducting well-publicized sobriety checkpoints, which can reduce alcohol-related traffic deaths by 20 percent. Officers need more training to conduct such checkpoints, and police departments should make conducting checkpoints a high priority. Federal transportation funding should be increased to help pay for sobriety checkpoints and to educate the public about the effort.

Drunk Driving Is A Serious Crime that Demands Serious Prevention and Enforcement

Drunk driving is the nation's most frequently committed violent crime, killing someone about every 30 minutes, according to the National Highway Traffic Safety Administration

5

Rebecca Kanable, "Driving Home a Message: DUI Is a Serious Crime, and Prevention and Enforcement Efforts Need Improvement," *Law Enforcement Technology* vol. 32, May 2005, p. 18. Copyright © 2005 Cygnus Business Media. All rights reserved. Reproduced by permission.

(NHTSA). Since 1980, the year Mothers Against Drunk Driving (MADD) was founded, alcohol-related traffic fatalities have decreased by 44 percent, from 30,429. Looking at the latest available statistics [as of 2005], the number of alcohol-related traffic fatalities is declining only slightly. In 2002 an estimated 17,419 people died; a year later 17,013 people died, according to NHTSA.

To further reduce the number of fatalities, change is needed in the criminal justice system and in the strategies being used. Among the organizations working for change are MADD, the Pacific Institute for Research and Evaluation (PIRE) and the Traffic Injury Research Foundation (TIRF). This article looks at their suggestions for change specifically in the areas of DUI prevention and law enforcement.

MADD's Recommendations

MADD, which has its national headquarters in Irving, Texas, earlier this year [2005] released its "Law Enforcement Leadership Summit Report" with recommendations for increasing the use of general deterrence strategies to stop drunk driving. Among the recommendations are: make the prevention of alcohol-related crashes a priority for law enforcement agencies and focus on general deterrence approaches that prevent alcohol-related traffic deaths and injuries.

> *Sobriety checks, if conducted properly and frequently, and they're well publicized, are the most effective strategy police can use to deter impaired drivers.*

A lot of officers measure success by looking at the number of criminals they catch, but James Fell, who serves on the National Board of Directors for MADD, says officers need to look at the number of alcohol-related crashes, and subsequent injuries and death.

ıing criminals doesn't take care of the problem with driving because we can't arrest enough people," he ꞓꞓꞓ ꞓre are too many violators out there."

Most Drunk Drivers Don't Get Caught

About 1.5 million drivers were arrested in 2002 for driving under the influence of alcohol or narcotics, according to NHTSA. Unfortunately, for every arrest there are 87 other instances of people driving over the legal blood alcohol concentration (BAC) limit, as noted in the 2000 NHTSA study, "Drinking and Driving Trips, Stops by Police, and Arrests: Analysis of the 1995 National Survey of Drinking and Driving Attitudes and Behavior."

More frequent and better publicized sobriety checks can cut impaired driving fatal crashes by 20 percent.

"We're not deterring enough people because many of these drivers know they're not going to get caught," says Fell, director of Traffic Safety and Enforcement Programs for PIRE in Calverton, Maryland. Although their driving is impaired and their risk of being involved in a crash is increased, these people don't speed and they don't weave down the road; they don't do things to attract the attention of law enforcement on routine patrol, he says. And officers can't just stop drivers without reason—they have to have probable cause—except when it comes to checkpoints.

Sobriety Checkpoints Are Key

A better strategy than focusing so much on the number of arrests is to use sobriety checkpoints to deter people from drinking and driving in the first place, Fell advises. Although there are some people, usually multiple offenders, who don't care about sobriety checkpoints or getting caught, in general when people hear that there are going to be checkpoints in their community, they are much more careful about their drinking and driving, he says.

"If impaired drivers go through a checkpoint and have to talk to police, especially police with passive alcohol sensors, they're going to get detected and investigated further," he says. "Then they'll be preliminarily breath-tested, and they'll be over the limit, and they'll get arrested—and they know that." Fell says checkpoints are going to deter people from drinking and driving because checkpoints are visible (it is very clear what they are for) and drivers think they will be detected by police if they are impaired.

In 10 states . . . sobriety checkpoints have been ruled illegal by the courts.

Surely, some people will find a way around checkpoints—checkpoints don't eliminate the problem—but Fell says they make a big dent in it. A summary of the research conducted by PIRE in 2004 found more frequent and better-publicized sobriety checks can cut impaired driving fatal crashes by 20 percent.

Sobriety Checkpoints Are Underutilized

PIRE research in 2000 found most law enforcement agencies don't use checkpoints enough because of misperceptions that checkpoints aren't productive or cost effective, and because of a lack of publicity about them in the local media.

"I think the mentality has to change," says Fell, the principal investigator for the PIRE report. "Many officers understand, but a lot of them don't. If they're out doing a checkpoint and they only arrest one driver in two hours, many officers say, 'The checkpoint wasn't fruitful. We didn't do anything good.' But they did. They deterred a lot of drivers from drinking and driving by just being out there and screening drivers."

In the earlier PIRE study, sponsored by the Insurance Institute for Highway Safety, Fell surveyed police agencies and found a half-dozen beliefs underlying most police agencies' reluctance to fully utilize checkpoints. For example, concerns about cost and manpower deter many departments. That's due to the belief that large numbers of officers must be used for checkpoints, but research sponsored by NHTSA found checkpoints using only three to five officers were effective.

Sobriety checkpoints should be part of routine enforcement in every community, Fell says. "They should be routinely conducted each Friday and Saturday night for two to three hours at different locations, and periodically on a weeknight and during happy hour times," he advises. . . .

Checkpoints Are Not Always Feasible

Despite the benefits of checkpoints, in some geographic areas, they are not feasible. Fell gives examples: It could be extremely dangerous to slow down high-speed vehicles on an interstate highway and back-up traffic. Checkpoints also may not be feasible in certain urban city areas where there is not enough space to set them up. Police need an area off the roadway where they can conduct further investigations after the initial screening of the drivers.

Passive sensors detect twice as many impaired drivers at checkpoints as officers do.

In 10 states (Idaho, Iowa, Michigan, Minnesota, Oregon, Rhode Island, Texas, Washington, Wisconsin and Wyoming) sobriety checkpoints have been ruled illegal by the courts. Alaska chooses not to conduct them. Fell urges change: "Sobriety checkpoints, if conducted properly and frequently, and they're well publicized, are the most effective strategy police can use to deter impaired drivers. There isn't anything else that comes close."

Fell's beliefs are further substantiated by an NHTSA experiment conducted in California in 1995. According to "Experimental Evaluation of Sobriety Checkpoint Programs," in four communities, highly publicized sobriety checkpoints were conducted. In two communities, publicized saturation and roving patrols were used. Alcohol-related crashes declined 28 percent in the checkpoint communities compared to a 17-percent decrease in the saturation patrol communities.

Passive Alcohol Sensors

If people know passive alcohol sensors are being used at checkpoints, that can be an even bigger deterrent because people know they will be detected if they have been drinking, Fell says, noting passive sensors detect twice as many impaired drivers at checkpoints as officers do. Because officers only have a few seconds to decide if a driver should be investigated further for suspicion of DUI, Fell says even the best officers don't detect all the impaired drivers that go through a checkpoint.

Passive alcohol sensors . . . sniff exhaled air from in front of a driver's face, in the same way an officer would smell a driver's breath. A press of a button activates a proprietary pump that draws an air sample into an electrochemical fuel cell that will indicate the presence of alcohol in a few seconds on a color-coded display when alcohol is present.

"Some impaired drivers get through checkpoints because the police don't detain them, so they think if they're polite and they don't reek of alcohol, they might get through a checkpoint. But with a passive sensor, they're going to get detected," says Fell, who worked at NHTSA as chief of research and evaluation for traffic safety programs, and managed the Fatality Analysis Reporting System (FARS). . . .

Training Is Essential

Because of the complexity of DUI cases, Herb Simpson, TIRF president and CEO, notes it is important that officers receive a comprehensive amount of training. From the detection of an impaired driver, to the apprehension and arrest, to the presentation of evidence in court, there's a lot to know, says Simpson. "It's important to recognize that drunk driving is one of the most complex criminal cases a police officer will be involved in," he says. "The statutes are monumental." Training offered nationwide varies. Some officers get very little training. Many agree there's a need for more uniformity and more standardization.

One area in need of detailed training is the application of standard field sobriety tests (SFSTs). If SFSTs are applied incorrectly, they become invalid evidence in court, notes Simpson, a previous board member of MADD Canada.

Learning to Spot Hard-Core Drunks

Another area where training could be improved is detecting drunk drivers, Simpson says. "Hard core drunk drivers, or high BAC drivers, usually have BAC levels that are two, three or four times the legal limit," he says. "Many are alcohol dependent and alcohol tolerant. You would not know that they had been drinking unless you could smell alcohol. They don't show any obvious signs of intoxication, and they know how to avoid detection because through their multiple offenses, they've encountered police many times. They do smart things such as making sure their vehicle registration and driver's license are clipped together so they don't fumble." This is obviously where a passive alcohol sensor would really help.

A third area for improved training is presenting evidence in court, Simpson says. "Many officers never go to court," he says. "They never testify. When they are called to testify, they are not very good at presenting the evidence." As a result, what could have been a slamdunk case, winds up being one that does not proceed, says Simpson, noting cross-training among officers and prosecutors helps educate and promote better understanding between the two groups. . . .

Advertising Can Help

The American public also needs to be better educated about drunk driving and its enforcement.

"When a community is aware of stepped-up enforcement efforts, drivers think twice about driving while impaired," according to a MADD press release on the "Law Enforcement Leadership Summit Report." One of the action plan's recommendations is promoting paid advertising to publicize enforcement efforts. "Sufficient resources must be allocated to make sure the word is out that drunk driving will not be tolerated," states the press release. . . .

Increased Funding Is Needed

For better DUI prevention and enforcement, funding for high-profile enforcement efforts needs to be increased, according to MADD's "Law Enforcement Leadership Summit Report." MADD notes alcohol-related traffic crashes in the United States cost the public an estimated $114.3 billion in 2000, including $51.1 billion in monetary costs and an estimated $63.2 billion in quality of life losses. MADD is seeking additional federal funding for law enforcement overtime, training and equipment to ensure the effective enforcement necessary to save lives and prevent injuries.

In a press release, Wendy Hamilton, MADD national president [2005], says, "If the nation is serious about stopping drunk driving, it is imperative that the highway funding bill includes increased resources for law enforcement to conduct checkpoints and for paid advertising to support these efforts. Tremendous progress has been made in increasing national seat belt usage by combining paid advertising with concentrated seat belt enforcement. MADD believes the combination of high-visibility enforcement and paid ads will go a long way to reducing alcohol-related death and injury."

Many people including officers and even high-ranking government leaders don't think of impaired driving as a crime or a serious crime. Driving drunk is a crime, a crime that claims a life every half-hour on average, according to NHTSA. That's a message that commanding officers need to drive home clearly. With sobriety checkpoints, passive alcohol sensors, advertising, improved training and other means, they can help reduce the injuries, deaths and property damage that occur as a result of this crime.

6

Sobriety Checkpoints Are Ineffective and Unconstitutional

Orange County Register Opinion-Editorial

The Orange County Register *is a daily newspaper in Southern California.*

Police should avoid conducting sobriety checkpoints for two reasons: They are not an effective way to reduce drunk driving, and they violate the Constitutional rights of American citizens. A very small percentage of the people randomly stopped by checkpoints are arrested as drunk drivers. Officers conducting roving traffic patrols catch far more drunk drivers than checkpoints do. The money and effort that police departments spend on checkpoints could be spent in much better ways. Checkpoints also violate the Fourth Amendment to the U.S. Constitution, which protects individuals from unreasonable search and seizure. The Supreme Court used flawed logic to allow sobriety checkpoints in the first place. It should reconsider its decision and realize that checkpoints undermine the public's essential right and need to keep government's power in check.

"Opponents of sobriety checkpoints tend to be those who drink and drive frequently and are concerned about being caught."

That's what Mothers Against Drunk [Driving] says. And that's correct, or as correct and logical as it is to say that only

Opinion-Editorial, "DUI Checkpoints of Dubious Value, Legality," *Orange County Register*, December 21, 2006. Copyright © 2006 Orange County Register. Reprinted by permission of the Orange County Register, copyright December 21, 2006.

pornographers oppose obscenity laws, communists oppose blacklists and terrorists oppose the Patriot Act.

At the risk of sounding like a bunch of defensive drunks, we'd like to point out as we enter DUI-checkpoint season that police should avoid the tactic for two reasons: They're relatively ineffective, and they violate our freedom under the Constitution.

First, the police can catch drunken drivers without checkpoints.

Police often are reluctant to set up checkpoints because they say it is inefficient and actually yields few arrests, according to studies by the Insurance Institute for Highway Safety and researcher H.L. Ross.

Roving Patrols Work Better

A much more effective approach is large-scale, roving patrols spread out over wide areas, which find more erratic drivers than clusters at a few set points.

A checkpoint by its nature involves arbitrary searches of people who have done nothing to arouse suspicion.

In the largest DUI checkpoint operation that's been studied, Tennessee set up 882 checkpoints throughout the state over the course of a year, stopping 144,299 drivers. The result of all that work: 773 DUI arrests.

To take an atypical but illustrative local example, a checkpoint run by the Irvine Police Department in 2004 and staffed by 27 officers and 24 others stopped 884 vehicles and made seven DUI arrests. By one comparison, Irvine officer Michael Hallinan made 137 DUI arrests that same year.

Proponents also argue that widespread checkpoints are a greater deterrent. As a paper put out last year by the Transportation Research Board has it, "highly publicized, highly visible, and frequent sobriety checkpoints reduce impaired driving fatal crashes."

This may well be true, but the reality is that few police departments have the funding to be omnipresent with frequent checkpoints, and, do we really want them to be?

Checkpoints Endanger Freedom

The second and crucial reason to avoid the tactic is that it endangers our freedoms under the Constitution, particularly regarding Fourth Amendment protections.

Current law was set in 1990, when the Supreme Court upheld DUI checkpoints in *Michigan v. Sitz*. Previously, checkpoints were allowed only for border control purposes.

In order to allow DUI checkpoints, the court had to ignore its own history and logic.

Americans have the Fourth Amendment right to be secure against "unreasonable searches and seizures." This means that police must have a reason—an "articulable and reasonable suspicion," in the court's words—to stop you. A checkpoint by its nature involves arbitrary searches of people who have done nothing to arouse suspicion.

Checkpoint proponents argue that these aren't really searches, that they're an administrative function to ensure traffic safety. But in 1976, the Supreme Court decided that "checkpoint stops are 'seizures'" under the Fourth Amendment.

The Court's Logic

If checkpoints, then, are seizures conducted without any reasonable suspicion, how could they square with the Fourth Amendment? Some argue that a car is not among the "persons, houses, papers, and effects" protected by the Fourth Amendment, or that because driving is a licensed activity, it's a privilege, not a right.

The court rejected that line of reasoning in *Delaware v. Prousein* (1979), stating that people "are not shorn of all Fourth Amendment protection when they step from their homes onto the public sidewalk; nor are they shorn of those interests when they step from the sidewalks into their automobiles."

If we would preserve our freedoms from the whims of the powerful, then we must defend the principles that restrain that power.

The court, then, grants that checkpoints are forbidden by the language of the Fourth Amendment, but allows them, anyway. How? It uses a balancing test, which is usually a good indication that one has left the ground of principle for that of preference.

Keeping Government in Check

The Fourth Amendment is not some social good to be balanced against other goods; it is a categorical prohibition of random searches. It supersedes federal law, state law, executive order and even international treaty. But the court imagines that it's on a par with a police department policy memo or the whim of a traffic agency official.

The balance to be taken here is not between the amenability of privacy and a worthy fight against drunken driving; it is between one dubious tactic in that fight and the weight of the explicit text of the Constitution.

Today's Supreme Court should backtrack to where its predecessor left its respect for the Fourth Amendment—*Martinez v. Sitz* would be a good place to start.

In American politics, the fundamental issue is the authority of the Constitution vs. the government power it's meant to check. If we would preserve our freedoms from the whims of the powerful, then we must defend the principles that restrain that power.

7

Ignition Lock Technology Will Reduce Drunk Driving

Glynn Birch

Glynn Birch is the national president and director of Mothers Against Drunk Driving (MADD), a national advocacy group for victims of drunk driving. His twenty-one-month-old son Court-ney was killed by a drunk driver in 1988.

An ignition interlock is a device that can prevent a vehicle from being started if the driver has consumed too much alcohol. All convicted drunk drivers—even first-timers—should be required to have an ignition interlock installed on their vehicle. The American public overwhelmingly supports requiring such a de-terrent to drunk driving. The main opponents of the idea are lawyers who profit from defending drunk-driving cases. Studies show that interlocks are highly reliable and that they signifi-cantly reduce repeat drunk-driving offenses. Interlock technology will keep people from driving drunk and will thereby save lives.

While we have made extraordinary progress over the last 26 years in the fight against drunk driving, it's still hard to believe that nearly 1,000 families get the knock at the door every month to be informed that a loved one has been killed in a senseless and preventable drunk-driving crash. This is why Mothers Against Drunk Driving [MADD] launched what it's calling the Campaign to Eliminate Drunk Driving to eradi-cate this devastating public health threat.

Glynn Birch, "Tapping Technology to Battle Drunk Driving; Ignition interlock devices can be a powerful tool in keeping repeat offenders from getting behind the wheel while intoxicated," *Business Week Online*, December 12, 2006. Copyright © 2006 by McGraw-Hill, Inc. Reproduced by permission.

Progress against drunk driving has stalled in recent years. And measures to stop drunks from driving, such as license suspension, aren't having the intended effect. For instance, two-thirds of those whose licenses are suspended for driving while under the influence of alcohol, or DUI, drive anyway.

That's why MADD—along with partners in federal and state government, law enforcement, the automobile industry, and distilled-spirits companies—believe the new campaign to eliminate, not reduce, drunk driving is the perfect antidote to the problem at hand.

Eighty-five percent of the public supports the mandatory installation of interlocks in the vehicles of repeat offenders.

Technology Should Play a Key Role

It's an audacious goal, but we know it can be done. The strategy involves using proven tactics, like high-visibility enforcement and grassroots mobilization, but the key to success relies on two important elements:

- The full implementation of current alcohol ignition interlock technologies, including laws that require alcohol ignition interlocks, which prevent a car from starting if a driver has had too much alcohol, for all convicted drunk drivers.

- The exploration and support of future advancements in technology that allow a vehicle to recognize if a driver is drunk and to stop the driver from operating that vehicle. This "smart technology" stops the drunk driver from harming or killing himself and other innocent people.

Public Supports Mandatory Interlock Devices

In a testament to Americans' intolerance of drunk driving, a recent poll found that 85% of the public supports the mandatory installation of interlocks in the vehicles of repeat offenders of laws against driving while intoxicated, or DWI, and 65% also support the mandatory installation of interlocks for first-time offenders. Americans also support advances in "smart technology" to prevent drivers from driving drunk by a 4-to-1 margin. The measure also has the support of the Distilled Spirits Council of the United States [a national trade association representing alcohol producers and marketers].

Of course, bold measures are usually met with opposition. In this case, some of the most vocal detractors of interlocks are, not surprisingly, the DUI defense attorneys whose clients face the loss of driving privileges and jail if they're caught driving drunk. At stake for the community, however, are the innocent people that could be killed or injured if the most effective tool to prevent drunk driving, especially among repeat offenders, is not used.

Offenders have significantly fewer repeat offenses while interlocks are on their vehicles.

If it were an episode of *Law and Order*, the scene would unfold like this: A man sits before the court, on trial for his third DUI offense. His attorney argues against a mandatory interlock. He says, "The technology is inaccurate, easily circumvented, and ineffective." He adds: "My client needs rehabilitation. He has a disease. He should be treated, not punished."

The defense attorneys, of course, are just doing their jobs— but often by distorting the facts and exploiting legal loopholes that sometimes result in rewarding crimes such as drunk driving.

Interlocks Are Highly Effective

Everyone is entitled to their own opinions on the matter, but they aren't entitled to their own version of the facts. There are some who still doubt the effectiveness of interlocks, citing a 2005 study by the California Motor Vehicles Dept. Opponents claim the study indicates that offenders who were sentenced to ignition interlock devices had an increased crash risk.

However, the failure in California, as several researchers including the study's authors have pointed out, isn't the fault of the devices—it's a failure of the program to get the devices installed on offenders' vehicles. Those studies that look at offenders who have interlocks installed find that these offenders have significantly fewer repeat offenses while interlocks are on their vehicles. There are many studies that prove the effectiveness of interlocks.

Interlock devices are up to 90% effective while installed in a vehicle, yet it's estimated that only one out of eight convicted drunk drivers each year currently gets the device, and the majority are repeat offenders. Research shows that the overwhelming majority of people arrested for drunk driving have driven drunk more than 50 times before their first arrest.

New Mexico, which since June, 2005, has mandated interlocks for first offenders, is the best model of successful judicial ignition interlock programs. The initial results are encouraging. Last year, alcohol-related fatalities in New Mexico dropped by nearly 12% from the previous year.

Interlock Technology Will Save Lives

Installing interlocks on all convicted drunk drivers' vehicles would save approximately 4,000 lives a year. I only wish my son could have been one of those lives saved. On May 3, 1988, Courtney was playing with his two older cousins at his grandmother's house. Hearing the alluring music of an ice cream truck, Courtney followed his cousins outside. That's when the offender's car came barreling down the street and hit Courtney at 70 mph, dragging his small body more than 150 feet before the car stopped. My son was killed instantly.

The drunk driver had a blood-alcohol level of .26 at the time of the crash and was driving with a revoked license and three prior DUI convictions. The driver would have been a prime candidate for an interlock. Instead, he killed my son and got 15 years in prison.

With current ignition interlocks and future technology, we finally have the ability to separate potential killers—drunk drivers—from their weapon, an automobile. We must use it.

Just like in a courtroom drama, the prosecution rests. The verdict: Interlocks and new technology will save lives.

8

Ignition Lock Technology Will Do Little To Reduce Drunk Driving

Lawrence Taylor

Lawrence Taylor is a former prosecutor, Fullbright law professor, and author of the legal textbook Drunk Driving Defense, *6th ed. His California DUI law firm is the largest of its kind in the nation.*

Interlock devices are not an appropriate way to discourage drinking and driving. The devices are inaccurate and can be easily fooled; they also present a dangerous distraction while driving. Studies show that installing interlocks on the cars of first-time DUI offenders does not change their likelihood of committing a second offense. Instead of monitoring first-timers, the focus should be on stopping hardcore problem drinkers and repeat offenders who cause most alcohol-related fatalities. Such drinkers are not deterred by the threat of jail because they have a disease: alcoholism. Society would be better served if such offenders were forced to undergo rehabilitation and treatment for their disease rather than serve time in jail.

Government statistics show that alcohol-related fatality figures have been essentially unchanged for the past decade—despite lowered blood-alcohol standards, Draconian penalties, roadblocks, legal presumptions of guilt, and other assaults on the Constitution.

Recognizing a failed effort, Mothers Against Drunk Driving [MADD] has unveiled with considerable fanfare its latest weapon in the "War on Drunk Driving": the ignition interlock device (IID). The device is not new, of course. It has been in use in many states for several years (with notably little success) and versions are being developed by Saab, Toyota and Nissan for possible installation in future car models as standard equipment. There are, however, two basic reasons this newest "answer" to the drunk driving problem will fail as well.

Device Is Ineffective

First, IIDs are inaccurate, easily circumvented, dangerous—and ineffective. Unlike the infrared spectroscopic breath instruments used by law enforcement, or even the less sophisticated handheld field units used by officers (deemed too inaccurate to be used in evidence), IIDs are primitive devices that are mounted along with the ashtray in the car's dashboard—and thus subject to contaminants, cigarette smoke, vibrations from the road, etc. In any event, an intoxicated person could easily have someone else breathe into the device, or simply borrow or rent another car. And because IIDs generally require periodic retesting of the driver while the car is underway, the risk from driver distraction alone poses a very real danger.

Most experts recognize that alcoholism is a disease, not a choice.

But how effective are IIDs in achieving MADD's goal of lowering fatalities? In a study of the devices' effectiveness in California, the state's Motor Vehicles Dept. came to the following conclusions:

- "The expected effect, that an IID order/restriction issued by the court would result in a lower rate of subsequent (driving under the influence) convictions, was not observed.

- "The risk of a subsequent crash was higher for drivers installing an IID, compared with drivers [who did not install] a device."

Study Shows Little Benefit

The study went on to say, "The results of this outcome study clearly show that IIDs are not effective in reducing DUI (driving under the influence of alcohol) convictions or incidents for first DUI offenders." It added, "Because there is no evidence that interlocks are an effective traffic safety measure for first DUI offenders, the use of the devices should not be emphasized."

The second reason the IID will fail is that, as with other attempts to bring down the alcohol-related fatality figures, the IID does not address the underlying problem. The risk of DUI-caused fatalities lies not with the social drinkers who represent the vast majority of drivers whose blood alcohol content is higher than .08%, most of whom are in the .08% to .15% range.

My own experience from prosecuting and defending thousands of people accused of DUI is that those who cause injury and death on our highways are usually fairly identifiable: the problem alcoholic. This client can usually be identified by two factors. First, the blood-alcohol level is very high, commonly over .20. Second, the client is a recidivist—that is, a repeat offender.

"Why not recognize a plea of 'not guilty by reason of alcoholism?'"

Thus, the first step is to identify the danger—the relatively small number of "problem drinkers"—and to stop filling our jails with social drinkers.

Jail Is Not the Answer

The second step is to decide what to do with this problem drinker/driver. Our present approach is purely punitive. But if we simply throw the alcoholic in jail for six months, what is accomplished? We've made the streets safe from him for six months—and on the day he gets out, he drives to the nearest bar and resumes his drinking. We have made no real progress: Our jails continue to burst at the seams, and the fatalities continue at their predictable levels.

I would suggest a rehabilitative approach rather than a punitive one, an approach that would actually take a step toward solving the problem rather than waiting for the vicious cycle to begin again. By now, most experts recognize that alcoholism is a disease, not a choice (the "choice" to drive, of course, is made by an inebriated person, and thus is a Catch-22). And you don't treat a disease with incarceration.

Offenders Need Treatment

We recognize legal incapacity due to mental disease. The plea or verdict is "not guilty by reason of insanity." The defendant is not simply set free, but is hospitalized for treatment of the disease until he is well. Why not treatment for problem drunk drivers who suffer from the (largely genetic) disease of alcoholism? In other words, why not recognize a plea of "not guilty by reason of alcoholism?" Again, this does not mean he "gets off." He will be ordered to undergo rehabilitative therapy. In serious cases, mandatory commitment to a rehabilitative facility may be appropriate.

The choice is fairly simple: Do you want vengeance, or safety? Would you prefer to have a chronic drunk driver off the road for a few months—or in control of his disease?

9

Teen License Restrictions Cut Drunk-Driving Deaths

Thomas S. Dee, David Grabowski, and Michael Morrisey

Thomas S. Dee is associate professor of economics and director of the Program in Public Policy at Swarthmore College in Pennsylvania. David C. Grabowski is associate professor of health economics in the Department of Health Care Policy at Harvard Medical School. Michael Morrisey is director of the Lister Hill Center for Health Policy at the University of Alabama.

In recent years, most states have adopted Graduated Driver Licensing (GDL) programs for new teen drivers. Such programs typically limit the driving activities of young people in several stages—such as not allowing them to drive with passengers or late at night—before granting them full driving privileges. While teens may chafe under such restrictions, a study by the authors shows that GDL programs save a significant number of lives each year. The authors also have found that the more restrictive the GDL program, the lower the rate of teen traffic fatalities, including those associated with drunk driving and alcohol use.

Over the last 8 years [during the 1997 to 2005 period], nearly every state has introduced graduated driver licensing (GDL) for teens. These new licensing procedures require teen drivers to advance through distinct stages where they are subject to a variety of restrictions (e.g., adult supervision, daytime driving, passenger limits). In this study, we present evi-

Thomas S. Dee, David C. Grabowski, and Michael A. Morrisey, "Graduated Driver Licensing and Teen Traffic Fatalities," *Journal of Health Economics* vol. 24, 2005, pp. 571–89. Copyright © 2005 Elsevier B.V. All rights reserved. Reproduced by permission.

dence on whether these restrictions have been effective in reducing traffic fatalities among teens. These evaluations are based on state-by-year panel data from 1992 to 2002. We assess the reliability of our basic inferences in several ways including an examination of contemporaneous data for older cohorts who were not directly affected by these policies. Our results indicate that GDL regulations reduced traffic fatalities among 15–17-year-olds by at least 5.6%. We also find that the life-saving benefits of these regulations were plausibly related to their restrictiveness. And we find no evidence that these benefits were attenuated [offset] by an increase in fatality risks during the full-licensure period available to older teens.

Our results indicate that these regulations reduce traffic fatalities among 15–17-year-olds by at least 5.6 percent.

In a recent report, the Centers for Disease Control and Prevention characterized improvements in motor vehicle safety as one of the 10 great public-health achievements of the 20th century. Over the last 3 decades, these gains have been particularly striking for young adults, the age group with the highest traffic fatality risk. More specifically, between 1975 and 1992, traffic fatality rates for 16–20-year-olds fell from 39 per 100,000 people to 28, a reduction of more than 25%.

These impressive gains are due to a diverse set of factors that includes state and federal policy initiatives like minimum legal drinking ages, mandatory seat-belt laws and drunk-driving regulations. However, since 1992, the annual traffic fatality rate of young adults has been remarkably stable at approximately 29 deaths per 100,000 people. Furthermore, despite the improvements of the last 30 years, traffic fatalities are still the leading cause of death among young adults, accounting for 6,277 deaths of 16–20-year-olds in 2002 alone.

States Introduce Graduated Licensing

Over the last 8 years [1997 to 2005], most states have responded to these public-health concerns by introducing graduated driver licensing (GDL) programs for young drivers. The signature feature of these regulations is that they require new drivers to advance through restrictive beginner and immediate phases before they can achieve full licensure. The fundamental intent of these programs is to encourage new drivers to acquire critical driving skills and experience in low-risk and monitored settings. In 1996, the state of Florida implemented the first GDL program in the United States. However, within just 6 years (i.e., by 2002), 38 states had introduced similar policies.

These new state-level licensing regulations have, arguably, become the premier policy initiative designed to improve traffic safety among young adults. However, largely because these policies are so recent, we know surprisingly little about their effects. In this study, we present new panel-based econometric evidence on the effects of GDL programs on teen traffic fatalities. . . .

In brief, our results suggest that GDL policies have been quite successful at reducing fatalities among teens. More specifically, our results indicate that these regulations reduced traffic fatalities among 15–17-year-olds by at least 5.6%. We find that these effects were monotonically [consistently] larger in states with more stringent policies. We do not find evidence that the cohorts subject to these new regulations had higher risks upon reaching full licensure. In the concluding section, we discuss the policy implications of these results in more detail.

How GDL Regulations Work

Graduated driver licensing (GDL) regulations differ from prior state licensing procedures largely because they establish three distinct licensing stages. However, the exact requirements associated with each stage vary across states in several dimensions. Nonetheless, a common feature of the initial "learning phase" is that young drivers can only drive in the presence of a licensed driver over the age of 21. States implementing GDL regulations often increased the age at which teens could obtain these initial permits as well. Furthermore, GDL reforms typically required that teens hold these permits for at least 6 months, during which the driver must log 30–60 hours of supervised driving. In the "intermediate phase" the young driver is allowed to operate a vehicle without supervision but only during daylight and early evening hours (e.g., only from 5 a.m. to 10 p.m.). In addition, they are typically allowed to have no more than one or two passengers in the car. The "full privileges phase" begins upon the successful completion of the earlier phases and at minimum ages as high as 18. . . .

Stringent GDL programs are markedly more effective in reducing teenage motor vehicle fatalities.

Effectiveness May Depend on Teen Compliance

The proponents of GDL regulations argue that these policies will save lives simply because they limit the amount of driving done by teen drivers, particularly in high-risk settings. Furthermore, these regulations may allow novice drivers to develop critical driving skills and experience under relatively safe and amenable conditions (e.g., daytime, with supervision). However, whether these new licensing procedures have actually been effective in reducing traffic fatalities ultimately depends on a number of factors. Most obviously, the degree of compliance and enforcement associated with these policies is likely to play an important role. In particular, some initial skepticism may be warranted because several key features of GDL regulations are clearly difficult to monitor and enforce (e.g., driver supervision, logged hours, passenger restrictions). This ambiguity implies that whether these regulations have an effect is an open, empirical question. . . .

Teen License Restrictions Save Lives

Graduated drivers licensing (GDL) programs attempt to promote traffic safety by providing new teenaged drivers with driving experience in progressively more independent situations. These driving regulations have been widely adopted by states over the last several years. This study evaluated the effects of these programs on teen traffic fatalities. Three major findings emerged from this analysis. First, GDL programs have been quite effective in reducing traffic fatalities among 15–17-year-olds. Our analysis indicates that the average GDL program led to a reduction in fatality counts of at least 5.6%. Second, our results also suggest that there are substantive differences in the effectiveness of alternative GDL programs. In particular, more restrictive policies (i.e., those characterized as "good" by the Insurance Institute for Highway Safety) appear to have reduced motor vehicle fatalities among 15–17-year-olds by 19%. The hallmarks of these particular GDL regulations are minimum time limits in the learner's stage, hours and passenger limits in the intermediate stage, and a minimum age at which one could have a full license. In contrast, "fair" programs, which lack some of these features, appear to have reduced teen traffic fatalities by only 6%. Some caution must be exercised in accepting the results for the "good" programs because only seven states implemented such policies, most of them recently.

More Restrictive Policies Are Most Effective

Nonetheless, the clear implication of these findings is that more stringent GDL programs are markedly more effective in reducing teenage motor vehicle fatalities. If teenage motor vehicle fatalities are to be reduced further, more stringent GDL programs appear to be one of the few successful tools available to policymakers. And, third, we investigated whether GDL regulations had any traffic-safety implications for teens when they reached full licensure. Our results provided preliminary evidence that they did not.

Rough calculations based on our estimates suggest that GDL regulations saved an appreciable number of young lives. More specifically, in 2002, there were 2,215 traffic fatalities among 15–17-year-olds in the 38 states that had implemented GDL. A 5.6% effect size implies that there would have been 131 additional teen fatalities in these states annually if they had not adopted these new licensing regulations. Furthermore, the 10 states in our sample that did not introduce GDL by the end of 2002 had 409 traffic fatalities among 15–17-year-olds. Our results imply that implementing GDL regulations would prevent at least 23 of these deaths annually.

GDL regulations have been highly effective at limiting the leading cause of fatalities among young people.

The Economic Perspective

From a policy perspective, these estimates can be used to conduct a "back-of-the-envelope" welfare analysis of the hypothetical adoption of GDL in the 10 states without such regulations by the end of 2002. A recent meta-analysis suggests that the value of a statistical life for prime-aged workers has a median value of about $7.3 million (in 2002 dollars) in the United States, implying that 23 young lives saved in 2002 would, at a minimum, be valued at $167.9 million. On the cost side, the administrative burden associated with GDL is fairly trivial in that these policies typically require (at most) one additional visit to the license examiner and only minimal additional law enforcement activities.

However, restricted driving during the late evening hours and with other teen passengers is probably the most significant cost of GDL, generating disutility among constrained teens and their parents. The magnitude of these costs is difficult to quantify. However, a crude but useful point of reference is to compare the dollar value of the lives in these 10 states ($167.9 million) to the number of 15–17-year-olds (i.e., 1.9 million individuals), who would be subjected to regulations in these states. These numbers imply that the dollar benefit, in terms of lives saved, per constrained teen is roughly $88. Many teens might be willing to pay this amount for the privilege of full licensure.

Does the Benefit Outweigh the Cost?

However, though this rough calculation suggests that GDL policies may generate costs in excess of their benefits, at least two caveats are worth bearing in mind. First, this exercise ignored the benefits from a reduction in injuries sustained in both fatal and non-fatal crashes. And, second, many policymakers and citizens are likely to reject such cost-benefit appraisals in favor of an unapologetically paternalistic view of the desirability of these licensing policies.

These cost-benefit questions are one of several that merit further scrutiny. Another question that should be revisited as additional data become available involves the relative effects of the most restrictive GDL regulations. Additional years of FARS [Fatality Analysis Reporting System, a census of all fatal motor vehicle crashes, collected by the National Highway Traffic Administration] data will also make it possible to identify more precisely whether GDL policies influenced traffic safety after full licensure and whether states can sustain the traffic-safety benefits of GDL policies beyond their initial implementation. Nonetheless, our results suggest that, despite these caveats, GDL regulations have been highly effective at limiting the leading cause of fatalities among young adults.

10

Designating a Driver
Is Not Enough

Peter Rothe

*Peter Rothe is senior associate and assistant professor in the
School of Public Health at the University of Alberta in Canada.*

*The often-recommended approach of designating a driver to
safely transport intoxicated friends does not work very well.
Many people do not choose a designated driver until drinking
has already begun, and the person chosen to drive typically still
drinks some alcohol. Designated drivers are often just the person
in the group who has had the least amount to drink—not a sober driver at all. In addition, designated drivers often face ha-
rassment, intimidation, or violence from intoxicated friends who
protest that they are in fact sober enough to drive themselves.
Recommending that students designate drivers is not enough.
School campuses should create prevention programs that focus
on how to help designated drivers deal with drunk friends.*

Campuses need to do more than suggest students pick a
designated driver to have effective programs to reduce
drunk driving, indicates new research from Canada.

"The idea of having a designated driver is a great one, but
it's problematic for many people," said Peter Rothe, lead investigator from the University of Alberta's Alberta Centre for Injury Control and Research. "The concept and practice of using
designated drivers should be re-thought to make it more effective."

Peter Rothe, "Designated Driver Programs Need To Be 'Re-thought,' researcher says,"
Campus Crime vol. 15, December 2005, p. 110. Copyright © 2005 Business Publishers,
Inc. Reproduced by permission.

According to Rothe's research, many people simply choose the least drunk person to be the designated driver. Also, designated drivers are sometimes reluctant to volunteer.

When a friend tries to stop someone from driving drunk, there is often a threat of a fight.

Rothe studied 1,000 Albertans aged 18 to 29 to determine their habits with respect to designated drivers. He found that most people used a designated driver (82.4 percent in urban areas and 75.5 percent in rural areas), but the designated drivers still drank. Nearly 20 percent of rural respondents said they didn't choose the designated driver until after people had started drinking.

Passengers Often Threaten Driver

A person chosen to be the designated driver often has a tough time convincing his charges to come with him. "One of the biggest surprises to me was how often designated drivers faced verbal and physical abuse from their friends and passengers," Rothe said. "When a friend tries to stop someone from driving drunk, there is often a threat of a fight. We heard from many people who said more often than not, they will back down and allow someone who has been drinking to get behind the wheel rather than risk a fight."

And while some shrink away from designated driving to avoid the prospect of conflict, others are okay with it. One respondent in the study said: "If they punch me in the face, they punch me in the face—they're drunk. I don't care."

Parents Set a Bad Example

The study also found that a significant percentage of young people were willing to drive while intoxicated, as they had seen their parents driving after a few drinks. Twenty-two percent of small city dwellers and 19 percent of large urban city dwellers were willing to drive after having several drinks because they had seen their parents drive after having three drinks within a four hour span. "It seems okay for 'good parents' to drink and drive if it's for a good reason," Rothe said.

Rothe recommends campus prevention programs that suggest designated drivers teach the designated driver "how to best deal with drunk drivers."

11

Driving Drunk Has a High Financial Cost

Christopher Solomon

Christopher Solomon is a freelance writer based in Seattle.

Drunk driving is a very expensive mistake. A typical DUI conviction costs the driver about $10,000, all told. Some of the expenses come right away, such as bail and towing fees when the arrest first happens. If the driver fights the charge, attorney fees alone can run several thousand dollars. A conviction necessitates paying numerous other fees and fines as part of the court sentence and license-restoration process. There are long-term costs as well. Significant insurance increases are inevitable, and rates can be affected for five years or more. Additionally, people who drive for a living may lose their jobs, and those in certain careers risk losing their professional licenses. Even if no one is injured, drunk driving is not worth the price.

If you need any more reasons not to drink and drive, consider this: A driving-under-the-influence conviction is a financial wrecking ball. A typical DUI costs about $10,000 by the time you pay bail, fines, fees and insurance, even if you didn't hit anything or hurt anybody.

The penalties are intended to be discouraging. Alcohol played a role in nearly 40% of U.S. automobile fatalities in 2005. That's 16,885 deaths, a figure nearly unchanged over the past decade, according to the National Highway Traffic Safety Administration.

Christopher Solomon, "DUI: The $10,000 ride home; A fine is just the start of what you'll pay for a drunken-driving conviction," *Moneycentral.msn.com* 2007. Reproduced by permission of MSN Money. www.moneycentral.msn.com.

But states are cracking down. The last of the 50 states have lowered their thresholds for DUI to 0.08% blood-alcohol content. Police arrested 1.37 million people last year for driving under alcohol's grip, about one in every 140 licensed drivers, the FBI says.

Many insurance companies will drop you even upon arrest, regardless of conviction.

But forget the humiliation and hassle for now. Forget the toll on lives. Just look at what a DUI does to your wallet:

Immediate Expenses

Bail. You'll have to shell out bail to get released after your arrest. **Cost: $150–$2,500.**

(Costs shown in this article are for first-time DUI offenders. Costs and penalties are often more severe if you're a repeat offender or your blood-alcohol content is above 0.15%.)

Towing. When you're arrested, your car gets towed. In some places, retrieving it costs only $100 or so. But Chicago, sensing a moneymaking opportunity, ensures it really hurts: The city charges about $1,200 for the first 24 hours and $50 for each additional day of storage, says Chicago DUI defense attorney Harold Wallin. If you can't afford to get your car after 30 days, the city auctions it and then comes after you with a civil judgment for the impoundment bill, if the car's sale didn't cover the fees. Some cities around Chicago are doing the same, Wallin says. **Cost: $100–$1,200.**

Insurance Will Increase Rates, May Cancel Policy

One of the biggest hits a drunken driver takes is in his insurance premiums.

"If you get a DUI conviction, it will likely affect your insurance rates for (at least) the next three to five years," says

Carole Walker, the executive director of the Rocky Mountain Insurance Information Association.

How much? "They could double, triple, even quadruple," Walker says. Some companies such as State Farm Insurance will move you to a portion of the company that handles higher-risk policies.

But "many insurance companies will drop you even upon arrest, regardless of conviction," says Steven Oberman, a Knoxville, Tenn., DUI attorney. And if your policy isn't renewed, you'll have to try to find insurance someplace else or see whether your state has an assigned-risk pool for insurance. Either way, you'll pay for it. For example: Illinois estimates that the high-risk insurance costs an additional $1,500 a year for three years, on average.

If you're convicted, you usually have to undergo an education or treatment program.

Why three years? Most insurance companies look at records for at least three years and sometimes for five years, Walker says. To begin rebuilding your reputation in an insurer's eyes, you have to keep your nose completely clean—no speeding tickets or other traffic citations.

But the financial impact of that DUI doesn't end after three years: You'll likely have to go as many as five more years, incident-free, to get back to the "preferred" status with the lowest premiums that you perhaps once enjoyed. In short, "it can be up to eight years afterward" that the DUI can affect, you, Walker says. Ouch. **Cost: $4,500 or more.**

Fighting a DUI Is Expensive

Legal fees. Attorneys might charge as little as $500 to enter a quick plea. But with so much at stake, many people accused of DUI fight the charge. That's when things start to add up.

Attorney Oberman says legal representation can cost anywhere from $2,500 to $25,000, depending on the rigor and complexity of the defense. But that's not the only fee. Oberman says a vigorous defense sometimes requires hiring an investigator ($1,000 to $3,000) to examine the arrest scene to poke holes in the arresting officer's story. There may be a need for expert witnesses who can testify about the accuracy, or lack thereof, of field sobriety tests ($3,000 and up). Usually, attorney Wallin says, fees are $2,000 to $3,000 for a trial on a first-offense case, although they can climb to $7,500 or more with some lawyers. "A lot of times, my fees are some of the smallest expenses that people have to worry about," given all the other costs, he says. **Cost: $2,000–$25,000.**

For many people who need to drive to and from their jobs—much less those who drive for their jobs—losing a license can be devastating.

Fines and Fees Add Up

Fines. Fines and court fees for breaking the law range from state to state, from a minimum of $300 in Colorado and $685 in Washington to as much as $1,200 in Illinois. "The fines have gone up dramatically over the last few years in Illinois," says Wallin. "A few years ago in Chicago, the typical DUI fine was about $300 on the first offense. And now it's $900 to $1,200." **Cost: $300–$1,200.**

Alcohol evaluation. An evaluation is usually required of anyone who is sentenced by the court for drunken driving. **Cost: $181 in Colorado, for example.**

Alcohol education and treatment. If you're convicted, you usually have to undergo an education or treatment program, especially if you want to get your license again. Treatment can vary hugely in scope and extent. **Cost: $350–$2,000 for basic treatment.**

License reinstatement fees. Once a driver has shown, by completing courses and treatment, that he deserves his license back, the state charges him for the reissue. **Cost: $60–$250.**

Additional fees. Colorado, for example, will slap you with myriad other fees:

$10 jail filing fee.

$78 Victim Assistance Fund payment.

$25 Victim Compensation Fund payment.

$90 for the Law Enforcement Assistance Fund.

$15 Brain Injury surcharge.

$25 Victim Impact Panel assessment.

If you had been particularly drunk, a judge might order that an ignition lock be placed on your car to test your breath and prevent your car from starting if you're intoxicated. In Tennessee, for example, this costs $65–$70 a month. **Cost: $308 and up.**

Many Long-Term Costs Are Hidden

Finally, there are several other costs that you need to remember:

Life-insurance-premium increases. With a DUI arrest or conviction, you could see an increase in your life-insurance bills because insurers may ask if your license has ever been suspended.

Lost time = lost money. People who've gotten DUIs report missing a lot of work (and therefore losing a lot of income) dealing with their mistake, as a result of court dates, community service and sometimes a jail sentence. That doesn't even count the lost free time.

Lose the license? Lose the job. For many people who need to drive to and from their jobs—much less those who drive for their jobs—losing a license can be devastating. And here's a shocker: In several states, including Washington, your license may be suspended for 90 days simply upon your arrest for DUI, regardless of whether you end up being convicted. If you're convicted, your license can be revoked for a year, or longer in other states, until you complete all the court's requirements and pay all fines.

No drunks in the cockpit or the ER. If you're a doctor, stockbroker, airline pilot, lawyer or nurse, a DUI conviction could affect the status of your professional license, Oberman said.

It's not good for the résumé. A DUI lingers on your criminal record for employers to see if they do a background check, harming your future job prospects. In Washington state, a DUI conviction also stays on your driving record for 14 years, and an employer can ask for and receive that information.

Expensive Mistake Has Social Cost, Too

So in the end, how much does a DUI cost?

The STOP-DWI Office in Erie County, N.Y., estimates that a drunken-driving conviction there costs $9,500—if no one is injured and there's no accident. Colorado estimates about the same thing.

Illinois' secretary of state pegs the amount closer to $10,600 but says the figure would be nearly $15,000, on average, if people counted the lost income from all the hassles.

Any way you slice it, it's a pricey mistake.

But the biggest thing that's lost isn't money, Oberman says. "The biggest thing here is the stigma that you get. Everybody looks at you and says, 'Yeah, he's the drunk driver.' And the stigma doesn't have a financial cost. But the stigma does have both a social cost and an employment cost."

12

Drunk Driving Paves the Way to Prison

Alfonso Castillo

Alfonso Castillo is a writer for Newsday.com.

In Suffolk, New York, a bill has been signed creating the crime of "aggravated vehicular homicide," in hopes of enforcing stricter punishments for those who cause deaths while driving drunk. Once the law is enacted, violators could face up to 25 years in prison. Some states have even tougher laws, such as Oklahoma and Washington, which issue sentences of up to life in prison for DWI homicides. Other states, like Texas, prefer "creative new ways" to prosecute drunk drivers using old laws.

Suffolk prosecutors were confident they could lock away Edwin Rodriguez for 25 years to life for killing three people in a fiery crash on New Year's Eve 1998 on the Long Island Expressway. And so, for the first time in 19 years, they charged a drunken driver with murder.

But as was the case the last time they charged murder in a drunken driving trial, jurors just didn't think the crime fit. Rodriguez eventually was sentenced to 5 to 15 years for second-degree manslaughter and is eligible for parole this year [2007]. Suffolk never again charged a suspected drunken driver with murder.

"We did everything we could," said Manhattan attorney Brian Rafferty, who prosecuted the case. "I'm sure if the district attorney had other options . . . he might have considered that instead."

Alfonso Castillo, "State Getting Stricter on Drunk Drivers," *www.newsday.com*, July 21, 2007. Reproduced by permission of the Los Angeles Times.

Aggravated Vehicular Homicide

Now, prosecutors do have another option. Gov. Eliot Spitzer signed into law earlier this week [in July 2007] a bill creating the crime of "aggravated vehicular homicide." New York is one of the growing number of states to create new laws that dole out stiffer punishments in the most egregious drunken driving homicides.

Historically, drunken drivers charged in fatal accidents have faced less jail time than other accused killers because they lacked the intent necessary to be charged with murder or even first-degree manslaughter.

In Oklahoma and Washington state, violators could face life in prison.

In rare cases, such as that of the Valley Stream man convicted in the wrong-way crash that killed Katie Flynn and limo driver Stanley Rabinowitz—second-degree murder can be charged, using the theory of "depraved indifference to human life." But lawyers often argue, and judges agree, that the intoxication itself prevents a defendant from forming the necessary state of mind for depraved indifference.

"To have that conversation where you explain that your loved one's killer might never go to jail is just heartbreaking," said Nassau District Attorney Kathleen Rice, who worked with state Sen. Charles Fuschillo (R-Merrick) in pushing for the new law. "The outrage is growing. It's an epidemic, and that's not hyperbole. It really is an epidemic, and people are recognizing the seriousness of it."

Case-by-Case Basis

But new laws being passed in several states—including New York—deal less with a defendant's mind-set and more with the context of a particular accident. They take into account aggravating factors, such as previous DWI convictions, high blood-alcohol level and number of victims. In New York, a defendant convicted of aggravated vehicular homicide will face a maximum of 25 years, once the law is enacted in November.

Prosecutors and lawmakers say legislation tailored toward the "worst of the worst" drunken drivers address the disparity between the elusive charge of murder, which is extremely difficult to prove in a DWI case—and the usual charge of second-degree manslaughter, which carries no mandatory jail time.

"There was a measurable gap between those two offenses," said Fuschillo, who drafted the new statute. "The prosecutors need a middle ground, and they felt strongly about that."

The legislation, approved by both houses of the State Legislature last month, was strongly supported by the family of Katie Flynn, the 7-year-old Long Beach girl who, along with Rabinowitz, was killed in July 2005 when she was struck head-on by drunken driver Martin Heidgen. He was convicted of murder—a rarity—after a trial wrought with legal obstacles.

Four other states have crimes punishable by up to 30 years in prison.

Defendants' Advocates Oppose Harsher Penalties

Although prosecutors and lawmakers say they have the support of the public, defendants' advocates say the trend toward harsher penalties for drunken drivers may be going too far, with little regard for justice, even-handedness and the rights of the accused. They say while locking up defendants may appease victims' families and help politicians' campaigns, they do little to curb drunken driving.

Albany defense lawyer Peter Gerstenzang said the irony of Heidgen inspiring New York's new law is that his trial showed that existing laws work just fine.

"This is not driven by logic or logical reasoning. It's driven by the passion of survivors," said Gerstenzang, a member of the National DUI Defense College and author of "Handling the DWI Case in New York."

"What we're suddenly saying is death caused by a car and a drunk driver is worse than death caused by similar conduct that doesn't involve a drunk driver."

DWI Homicides Could Equal Life in Prison

According to data compiled in 2005 by the American Prosecutors' Research Institute, only six other states have tougher laws for DWI homicides than New York. In Oklahoma and Washington state, violators could face life in prison. Four other states have crimes punishable by up to 30 years in prison. Seven states, besides New York, carry up to 25-year sentences.

During the past five years, other states, including Illinois and Arizona, have enacted aggravated DUI laws, all carrying stiffer penalties than previous laws.

Had the new statute existed, Suffolk District Attorney Thomas Spota could have used it against Karen Fisher. She had a blood-alcohol level more than three times the legal limit and was twice before arrested for drunken driving when she killed retired priest William Costello in East Hampton last year. Instead, she pleaded guilty to second-degree manslaughter and is serving 4 to 12 years in prison.

"These enhanced penalties are far more appropriate for defendants convicted of taking the lives of innocent people while drunk behind the wheel," Spota said in statement. "Perhaps the prospect of up to 25 years in an upstate prison will prove to be a sufficient deterrent and save lives."

Creative Prosecution

In other states, such as Texas, prosecutors are finding creative new ways to prosecute drunken drivers using old laws. Harris County prosecutor Warren Diepraam discovered a way to charge repeat drunken drivers under the state's "felony murder" law, which states that if anyone dies during the commission of a felony, it's murder.

While most states use a similar statute to charge murder in cases where someone dies during a violent crime, Diepraam argued a third drunken driving offense was a felony in itself. He said about 10 defendants have been prosecuted under the statute since its conception in 2003.

Although Diepraam said the public has praised prosecutors' tough stance, defense attorneys say they are noticing knee-jerk reactions to any crime involving alcohol—even where alcohol may not be a factor. Attorneys gave as an example an intoxicated driver who hits a pedestrian who darts into the street.

"It's difficult for prosecutors to remember that they are not there for the purpose of succumbing to public outcry," said Knoxville, Tenn., lawyer Stephen Oberman, of the National Association of Criminal Defense Lawyers's DUI committee. "Their job is to do justice. . . . It's not simply to put somebody in jail or try to bring the most serious charge against them."

13

Celebrity Drunk-Driving Arrests Should Disturb, Not Entertain

Louis Wittig

Louis Wittig is a media writer in New York.

The list of celebrities who have had drunk-driving arrests is a long one. The American public should be bothered by this, but it isn't. Americans seem to treat celebrity DUI's as entertainment, rather than serious crimes. The public is more concerned with what the celebrity was wearing or saying when they got arrested than the fact that they could have hurt someone while driving under the influence. The reason for this is that the public depends on celebrities for the illusion of a trouble-free life. Celebrities engage in such risky behavior and face few consequences from their fans because the public expects them to be zany and eccentric. It is up to the American public to stop tacitly condoning such behavior.

"Hollywood is out of touch with mainstream America."

I love saying that. Especially when I'm midriff deep in the plain-folk American things I do every day: eating apple pies baked in the shape of individual states, shopping for the brand of brake pad that reminds me most of Ronald Reagan, or taking a break from raising a barn just to recite the Pledge of Allegiance. And honestly, it's never bugged me that it's not entirely true.

This isn't as fun to say, but Hollywood mostly obeys the same commandments they do in Peoria. For example, in Hollywood, thou shalt not kill. In Hollywood, adopting underprivileged children is good. (There's even a supplemental child-country-of-origin bonus point system by which hot-bistro reservations are allotted.) Interrupting your comedy routine to hurl fevered racist insults at nearby strangers is also bad in Tinseltown. And—this holds equally true for sitcom leads and longshoremen—leaking a sex tape of yourself can greatly complicate (and, occasionally, greatly enhance) your career. But one issue where Hollywood's moral instincts really are out of sync is when it comes to drunk driving.

For some strange reason, we treat celebrity DUIs as entertainment, like some real-life version of Law & Order. *Arrest, Rehab. Repeat.*

Long List of Celebrity Offenders

Lots [of] bad things happen when ordinary Americans drive drunk. Fines. Prison sentences. Deaths. (There were 16,885 DUI-related deaths in 2005.) When celebrities drive drunk—and there's a swerving parade of them: Paris Hilton, Tim Allen, Haley Joel Osment, Rip Torn, Tracy Gold, Nick Carter, Andy Dick, assorted reality TV stars, that cook character from *The Sopranos*, Mike Tyson, Gus Van Sant, (Britney Spears hasn't yet, but the odds that she will on WagerWeb.com are such that if you bet she will be caught, and you "win," you actually lose money). But the closest these celebrities come to disgrace is a preciously befuddled mug shot. (Oh, the humanity.)

The crime itself, which is more or less the equivalent of attempted criminally negligent homicide, takes a backseat to the hairdo. When Nicole Richie was popped—driving the wrong way down a six-lane highway, high on vicodin [a painkiller], with her headlights off in the middle the night—the gossip blogs were, understandably, agog. But not for the reason you think. It was because the police report revealed that the scary-skinny Richie weighed just 85 pounds.

Misplaced Priorities

For some strange reason, we treat celebrity DUIs as entertainment, like some real-life version of *Law & Order*. Arrest. Rehab. Repeat. With this sort of stultifying line-up, DUI producers are under constant pressure to go further. Earlier this year *Lost* co-stars Michelle Rodriguez and Cynthia Watros left the same party, driving different cars, and were arrested on the same road just minutes apart—simultaneously inventing and taking the gold in women's synchronized drunk driving.

Murder and racism are crimes of wrath and hatred. But drunk driving is, fundamentally, a crime of carelessness.

Yet instead of becoming outcasts, society seems to look playfully at these offenders. Consider the great Mel Gibson scandal. After being arrested for DUI, what people were really outraged about were his drunken, anti-Semitic ramblings. On every channel, for days, people clucked their tongues. Condemnations came from every corner and people went back through his old movies looking for anti-Semitic subtext. Important industry leaders were offended. And no one even seemed to remember that he had been caught with a blood-alcohol level of 0.12. Forget what Gibson said; isn't it just a little worse that he could have killed someone?

Public Looks the Other Way

I can already hear the grumbling. [President] George W. Bush and [Vice President] Dick Cheney both have DUIs on their record(s) so why hold Nicole Richie to a higher standard? But consider that in 2000, before his DUI arrest hit the press, Bush was leading in the polls. Shortly afterwards, he lost the popular vote. Now try to imagine how many Americans avoided seeing *The Lake House* specifically because Keanu Reeves drove drunk in 1993.

For some reason, celebrities get a special pass on DUIs. But it's a pass that we, their adoring public, give them. Why?

A hypothesis: We follow celebrities' personal lives so intently because they create for us the perfect illusion of a carefree life. Celebs are rich and beautiful and loved. You never actually see them working. The problems that vex them? Wardrobe malfunctions. Petty break-ups. Slightly embarrassing rumors. For most mainstream Americans, just soaking in the possibility of this unbothered life is mild rapture.

Murder and racism are crimes of wrath and hatred. But drunk driving is, fundamentally, a crime of carelessness. (And until someone gets badly hurt, an apparently harmless one.) We can't really blame celebrities for doing it. Doing untroubled, egocentric things—that's what we love them for.

Sure, Hollywood is out of touch with mainstream America when it comes to drunk driving. But maybe that's what its audience demands.

Organizations to Contact

The editors have compiled the following list of organizations concerned with the issues debated in this book. The descriptions are derived from materials provided by the organizations. All have publications or information available for interested readers. The list was compiled on the date of publication of the present volume; the information provided here may change. Be aware that many organizations take several weeks or longer to respond to inquiries, so allow as much time as possible.

Advocates for Highway and Auto Safety
750 First St. NE, Ste. 901, Washington, DC   20002
(202) 408-1711 • fax: (202) 408-1699
e-mail: advocates@saferoads.org
Web site: www.saferoads.org

Advocates for Highway and Auto Safety is an alliance of consumer, health, and safety groups and insurance companies that seek to make U.S. roads safer. The alliance advocates the adoption of federal and state laws, policies, and programs that save lives and reduce injuries, including those that prevent drunk driving. On its Web site the organization publishes fact sheets, press releases, polls, and reports, as well as links to legislative reports and testimony on federal legislation involving traffic safety, including the problem of drunk driving.

American Beverage Institute (ABI)
1090 Vermont Ave. NW, Ste. 800, Washington, DC   20005
(202) 463-7110
Web site: www.americanbeverageinstitute.com

ABI is a restaurant trade association that unites wine, beer, and spirits producers with distributors and on-premise retailers. The institute is dedicated to protecting the on-premise dining experience, which often includes the responsible consumption of alcoholic beverages. ABI conducts research and public education programs to demonstrate that many adults who enjoy alcoholic beverages away from their homes are reasonable, law-abiding Americans and counters campaigns to reduce the consumption of alcohol by sensible adults. ABI publishes reports, including *In Their Own Words: The Traffic Safety Community on the Real Drunk Driving Problem—and Its Solutions, The .08 Debate: What's the Harm?* and *Roadblocks: Targeting Responsible Adults.*

Boaters Against Drunk Driving (BADD)
344 Clayton Ave., Battle Creek, MI   49017-5218
(269) 963-7068 • fax: (269) 963-7068
e-mail: SafeBoating@BADD.org
Web site: www.badd.org

BADD is dedicated to promoting safe, sober, and responsible boating throughout the United States and Canada. Through its judicial watch projects, BADD monitors cases of individuals charged with boating under the influence of alcohol; BADD publishes the progress of these cases to demonstrate to the boating community and the general public that state boating officials, legislators, prosecutors, and courts all consider boating under the influence a very serious crime. BADD's Web site includes statistics, charts, and articles concerning the dangers of boating under the influence, including "Drinking on Your Boat—It Really Does Matter."

Center for Substance Abuse Prevention (CSAP)
Substance Abuse and Mental Health Services Administration
Rockville, MD   20852
(800) 729-6686 • fax: (240) 221-4292
Web site: http://ncadi.samhsa.gov

The CSAP leads the U.S. government effort to prevent alcoholism and other substance abuse problems among Americans. Through the NCADI, the center provides the public with a wide variety of information concerning alcohol abuse, including the problem of drunk driving. Its publications include the bimonthly *Prevention Pipeline*, the report *Impaired*

Driving Among Youth: Trends and Tools for Prevention, brochures, pamphlets, videotapes, and posters. Publications in Spanish are also available.

Century Council
1310 G St. NW, Ste. 600, Washington, DC   20005
(202) 637-0077 • fax: (202) 637-0079
e-mail: moultone@centurycouncil.org
Web site: www.centurycouncil.org

Funded by leading U.S. alcohol distillers, the Century Council is a not-for-profit national organization committed to fighting underage drinking and reducing alcohol-related traffic crashes. The council promotes legislative efforts to pass tough drunk-driving laws and works with the alcohol industry to help servers and sellers prevent drunk driving. Its interactive CD-ROM, *Alcohol 101*, provides "virtual" scenarios to help students make sensible, fact-based decisions about drinking alcohol.

Insurance Institute for Highway Safety
1005 N. Glebe Rd., Ste. 800, Arlington, VA   22201
(703) 247-1500 • fax: (703) 247-1588
Web site: www.hwysafety.org

The Insurance Institute for Highway Safety is a nonprofit research and public information organization formed by auto insurers. The institute conducts research to find effective measures to prevent motor vehicle crashes, including those that result from drunk driving. On its Web site, the institute publishes information on the results of its research, including press releases, a table of each state's impaired driving laws, the institute's rating of those laws, and a bibliography of articles on highway safety topics, including drunk driving. The institute publishes a newsletter, *Status Report*, and makes the current issue available on its Web site.

Mothers Against Drunk Driving (MADD)
511 E. John Carpenter Freeway, Ste. 700, Irving, TX   75062
800-GET-MADD (438-6233) • fax: (972) 869-2206/07

Web site: www.madd.org

A nationwide grassroots organization, MADD provides support services to victims of drunk driving and works to influence policy makers by lobbying for changes in legislation on local, state, and national levels. MADD's public education efforts include a *Rating the States* report, which draws attention to the status of state and federal efforts against drunk driving. On its Web site MADD publishes statistics, fact sheets, and reports on drunk driving and drunk-driving laws, including "Costs of Impaired Driving in the United States by State." MADD publishes numerous brochures and pamphlets about the dangers of drunk driving as well as the semiannual magazine *Driven*, recent issues of which are available on its Web site.

National Commission Against Drunk Driving (NCADD)
1900 L St. NW, Ste. 705, Washington, DC   20036
(202) 452-6004 • fax: (202) 223-7012

NCADD comprises public and private sector leaders who are dedicated to minimizing the human and economic losses resulting from alcohol-related motor vehicle crashes by making impaired driving a socially unacceptable act. Working with private sector groups and federal, state, and local officials, NCADD develops strategies to target the most intractable groups of drunk drivers: underage drinkers, young adults, and chronic drunk drivers. The commission's publications include research abstracts, traffic safety fact sheets, and reports.

National Highway Traffic Safety Administration (NHTSA)
Impaired Driving Division, Washington, DC   20590
(888) 327-4236
e-mail: hotline@nhtsa.dot.gov
Web site: http://stopimpaireddriving.org

The NHTSA allocates funds for states to demonstrate the effectiveness of visible enforcement initiatives against drunk driving. The mission of its Impaired Driving Division is to save lives, prevent injuries, and reduce traffic-related health-care and economic costs resulting from impaired driving. On its Web site, NHTSA provides program guides that include sample public service announcements, camera-ready art, and information on how to prepare local media campaigns about drunk driving. The organization also publishes reports on drunk-driving issues, including *The Nation's Top Strategies to Stop Impaired Driving*, and *Alcohol-Related Fatalities in 2004, with State-by-State Listing*, which are available on its Web site.

National Motorists Association (NMA)
402 W. Second St., Waunakee, WI   53597-1342
(608) 849-6000 • fax: (608) 849-8697
e-mail: nma@motorists.org
Web site: www.motorists.org

Founded in 1982, the NMA advocates, represents, and protects the interests of North American motorists. The NMA supports drinking-and-driving regulations based on reasonable standards that differentiate between responsible, reasonable behavior and reckless, dangerous behavior. The NMA does not support "zero tolerance" concepts, nor does it endorse unconstitutional enforcement and judicial procedures that violate motorists' rights. On its Web site the NMA provides access to articles and reports, including "The Anti-Drunk Driving Campaign: A Covert War Against Drinking," "Back Door to Prohibition: The New War on Social Drinking," and "The Flawed Nature of Breath-Alcohol Analysis."

Recording Artists, Actors & Athletes
Against Drink Driving (RADD)
4370 Tujunga Ave., Ste. 235, Studio City, CA   91604
(818) 752-7799 • fax (818) 752-7792
e-mail: robert.pineda@radd.org
Web site: www.radd.org

RADD is an international nonprofit organization made up of prominent musicians, celebrities, and media partners working to create positive attitudes about safe driving. Founded in

1986, RADD advocates using designated drivers and seatbelts and emphasizes safe driving through control behind the wheel. RADD's messages are non-judgmental, hip, and positive, and its goal is to make responsible behavior the norm. RADD's Web site includes a link to screening kits for the HBO documentary "Smashed: Toxic Tales of Teens and Alcohol."

Responsibility in DUI Laws, Inc. (RIDL)
PO Box 97053, Canton, MI   48188
e-mail: info@ridl.us
Web site: www.ridl.us

A group of concerned citizens, RIDL believes that some drunk-driving laws criminalize and punish responsible drinkers while having little or no effect on drunk driving. Its goal is to educate the public and lawmakers about the misdirection of drunk-driving laws, to take steps necessary to get these laws repealed, and to provide alternatives to reduce drunk driving. On its Web site RIDL includes personal stories of victims of drunk-driving laws, statistics, and reports, including "Behind the Neo-Prohibition Campaign," and "DUI Laws: Out of Control—This Nightmare Can Happen to You."

Students Against Destructive Decisions (SADD)
255 Main Street, Marlborough, MA   01752
(877) SADD-INC • fax: (508) 481-5759
Web site: www.sadd.org

Founded in 1981 as Students Against Driving Drunk, SADD is a school-based organization dedicated to addressing the issues of underage drinking, impaired driving, drug use, and other destructive decisions that harm young people. SADD seeks to provide students with prevention and intervention tools that build the confidence needed to make healthy choices and behavioral changes. On its Web site, SADD provides sample public service announcements and "Contracts for Life," which facilitate communication between teens and their parents about potentially destructive decisions related to alcohol, drugs, and peer pressure. SADD publishes a semiannual newsletter, *Decisions*, recent issues of which are available on its Web site.

Traffic Injury Research Foundation (TIRF)
171 Nepean St., Ste. 200, Ottawa, ON   K2P 0B4
  Canada
(613) 238-5235 • fax: (613) 238-5292
e-mail: tirf@trafficinjuryresearch.com
Web site: www.trafficinjuryresearch.com

Founded in 1964, TIRF is an independent road safety institute that seeks to reduce traffic-related deaths and injuries in Canada by designing, promoting, and implementing effective programs and policies based on sound research. TIRF publications include brochures, the *TIRF Bulletin,* and technical reports, including *About Alcohol Ignition Interlocks 2007* and *The Road Safety Monitor 2006: Drinking and Driving,* which are available on its Web site.

Bibliography

Books

Robert T. Ammerman   *Prevention and Societal Impact of Drug and Alcohol Abuse.* Mahwah, NJ: Lawrence Erlbaum Associates, 1999.

Dennis Bjorklund   *Drunk Driving: A Survival Guide for Motorists.* Iowa City: Praetorian Publishers, 2000.

Richard Bonnie and Mary Ellen O'Connell   *Reducing Underage Drinking: A Collective Responsibility.* National Research Council (U.S.) Committee on Developing a Strategy to Reduce and Prevent Underage Drinking, 2004. Washington, DC: National Academies Press, 2004.

Alan Cavaiola and Charles Wuth   *Assessment and Treatment of the DUI Offender.* Binghamton, NY: Hawthorn Press, 2002.

Deborah Chrisfiels   *Drinking and Driving.* Mankato, MN: Crestwood House, 1995.

Karen Goodman and Kirk Simon   *The Safe Road Home: Stop Your Teen from Drinking and Driving.* New York: Sterling, 2005.

Jeff Herten   *An Uncommon Drunk: Revelations of a High-Functioning Alcoholic.* iUniverse: Lincoln, NE, 2006

James Jacobs   *Drunk Driving: An American Dilemma.* Chicago: University of Chicago Press, 1992.

Chris Overbey   *Drinking and Driving War in America.* Morrisville, NC: Lulu Press, 2006.

Frank A. Sloan, ed.   *Drinkers, Drivers, and Bartenders: Balancing Private Choices and Public Accountability.* Chicago: University of Chicago Press, 2000.

Periodicals

Brandy Anderson   "Congress Passes National .08 BAC Law," *Driven*, Fall 2000.

Radley Balko   "Back Door to Prohibition: The New War on Social Drinking," *Policy Analysis*, December 5, 2003.

Andrew Blankstein and Megan Garvey   "Paris Hilton Must Serve 45 Days in Jail," *Los Angeles Times*, May 5, 2007.

Sam Bresnahan   "Breathalyzers vs. Teen Drunk Driving—Parents Trying Ignition-Locking Devices in Vehicles as Deterrents," www.cbsnews.com, May 17, 2006.

"MADD Struggles to Remain Relevant," *Washington Times*, August 6, 2002.

Piotr C. Brzezinski   "Drunk Until Proven Innocent," *The Harvard Crimson*, November 21, 2006.

Tim Coffey

"MADD Tailors Its Message to Latino Community," *San Diego Business Journal*, vol. 21, no. 27, 2000.

Robert Fancher

"Drinking and Driving Remains a Serious Threat to Teen Safety," www.libertymutual.com, May 21, 2001.

"Drinking and Driving: When a Drunk Driver Smashed His Car into the Vehicle Robert Fancher Was Riding in, the Accident Changed the Course of Robert's Life," *Scholastic Choices*, September 1, 2003.

Michael D. Greenberg, et al.

"How Can Repeat Drunk Drivers Be Influenced to Change? Analysis of the Association Between Drunk Driving and DUI Recidivists' Attitudes and Beliefs," *Journal of Studies on Alcohol*, vol. 65, 2004.

David Hafetz

"Chasing Hope: Her Old Life Vanished in Flames. Now, Guided by a Tenacious Will and Her Father's Devotion, Jacqui Fights Every Day to Recover," *Austin American-Statesman*, May 12, 2002.

Sylvia Hsieh

"Case Gives New Life to Defense that DUI Test Unfair to Women," *Lawyers Weekly USA*, April 28, 2003.

Dan Levine

"Wasted: Why Our Drinking Laws Will Never Work," *Hartford Advocate*, August 24, 2000.

Jeanne Mejeur   "Way Too Drunk to Drive: About 48 People a Day Are Killed by Drunk Drivers; Some of Those Drivers Are Extremely Drunk," *State Legislatures*, vol. 31, December 2005.

Jeanne Mejeur   "Still Driving Drunk: Strict Drunk Driving Laws Don't Do Much Good Unless They Are Vigorously Enforced," *State Legislatures*, vol. 29, December 1, 2003.

Llewellyn H. Rockwell Jr.   "Legalize Drunk Driving," Ludwig von Mises Institute, www.mises.org, November 2000.

Sheila Sarkar, et al.   "Who Uses Safe Ride Programs: An Examination of the Dynamics of Individuals Who Use a Safe Ride Program Instead of Driving Home While Drunk," *American Journal of Drug and Alcohol Abuse*, vol. 31, 2005.

USA Today   "Hardcore Drinkers Are a National Plague," , November 1, 2005.

Ralph Vartabedian   "Drunk-Driving Reforms Stir Safety Debate," *Los Angeles Times*, October 2, 2003.

Matthew L. Wald   "A New Strategy to Discourage Driving Drunk," *New York Times*, November 20, 2006.

Jiang Yu   "Drinking-Driving and Riding with Drunk Drivers Among Young Adults: An Analysis of Reciprocal Effects," *Journal of Studies on Alcohol*, September 1, 1999.

Index

Tripp, Pam (parent of victim),
24–26

U

United States v. Martinez-Fuerte,
50
U.S. Constitution. *See* Constitutional rights' violations; Fifth
Amendment violations; Fourth
Amendment violations
U.S. Supreme Court, 34, 47, 49–51

V

Vehicles
confiscation, 11, 14, 36
safety, 15, 31
Victims, 18–29, 55–56, 78, 79, 80

W

Washington (state)
drunk driving costs, 74, 75–76
drunk driving punishments,
77, 80
Washington, D.C., drunk driving
laws, 33, 36
Watros, Cynthia, 84
Witnesses, costs of, 74
Wittig, Louis, 82

Y

Young people. *See* Teenagers

Z

Zero tolerance policies, 33, 36